I hope you
enjoy the book

Marilyn

The Divine Comedy 2.0

Revisiting the Afterlife

Marilyn Jess

ARCHWAY
PUBLISHING

Scripture taken from the King James Version of the Bible.

Scripture quotations marked RSV are taken from the Revised Standard Version of the Bible, copyright 1946, 1952, 1971 by the Division of Christian Education of the National Council of the Churches of Christ in the USA. Used by permission.

Archway Publishing books may be ordered through booksellers or by contacting:

Archway Publishing
1663 Liberty Drive
Bloomington, IN 47403
www.archwaypublishing.com
1 (888) 242-5904

Because of the dynamic nature of the Internet, any web addresses or links contained in this book may have changed since publication and may no longer be valid. The views expressed in this work are solely those of the author and do not necessarily reflect the views of the publisher, and the publisher hereby disclaims any responsibility for them.

Any people depicted in stock imagery provided by Thinkstock are models, and such images are being used for illustrative purposes only. Certain stock imagery © Thinkstock.

ISBN: 978-1-4808-4210-6 (sc)
ISBN: 978-1-4808-4211-3 (hc)
ISBN: 978-1-4808-4212-0 (e)

Library of Congress Control Number: 2017903873

Print information available on the last page.

Archway Publishing rev. date: 03/23/2017

Acknowledgement:

I am deeply indebted to Dante Alighieri for allowing me to channel him, and I am especially grateful to him for writing the first draft of The Divine Comedy 2.0.

Preface:

The *Divine Comedy* by Dante Alighieri stands as one of our greats in classical literature, along with Homer's *Illiad* and *Odyssey*, Virgil's *Aeneid*, the works of Shakespeare and many other treasures of Western culture. These works are not only examples of exquisite written art, but they are historical documents which have value today because of their universal themes that echo our modern relationships and anxieties. In reading them one is often surprised at the humanity of the central characters.

The *Divine Comedy* was written in the early 1300's in the Tuscany province of Italy during a traumatic time. Great controversy raged within the Church as schisms were threatened and the roles of clerics versus secular politicians were blurred. Far from being a secluded poet dreaming up a fanciful story about being led through Hell, Purgatory and Heaven, Dante was caught up in the thick of the action at the time. Florence Italy, his home city, was a boiling cauldron of intrigue and tensions with a civil war brewing between two factions, the Guelphs and the Ghibellines over the separation of Church and State. Dante himself fought as a soldier in conflicts which cost tens of thousands of lives. He also was involved in Florentine politics as a magistrate and a member of the Apothecary's guild. His political activities caused him to be tried in absentia while on a diplomatic mission, and sentenced to exile from Florence.

Not only a revolutionary in local politics, Dante was an artistic revolutionary. Schooled in Latin and Greek classical works, the intellectual treatises and poetry of his time were traditionally done in Latin. Dante wrote his masterpiece plus numerous other poems in the Italian vernacular which brought criticism from other writers of his day.

The story line of the *Comedy* is Dante's journey through the three realms of the afterlife, as understood by Catholic doctrine. Dante is led through Hell and Purgatory by Virgil, a Roman poet whom Dante deeply admired. A childhood sweetheart named Beatrice, who died quite young, leads Dante through Heaven since he considered her to be the epitome of beauty and virtue. In the *Comedy* Dante liberally mentions political allies and foes for example, he places his nemesis – Pope Boniface VIII – in the lowest ring of Hell near Satan Himself. Poet, political activist, soldier, homeless exile – Dante remains alive and vital through his masterpiece.

In writing this book I relied heavily on John Ciardi's translation. I, unfortunately, do not speak Italian myself. Therefore, I highly recommend Professor Ciardi's rendering of the *Comedy* because he not only translates Dante, but he also captures as much of Dante's rhyme scheme and meter as a translated copy will allow. Not only is Ciardi's 1957 translation poetically elegant, but he has copious footnotes and comments with his text which make the many historical facts understandable to the modern reader. Hopefully the *Divine Comedy 2.0* can stand on its own as enjoyable reading. But, if further insight is desired into the classical work on which this book is based, I did follow Dante's story line enough so that hopefully the original *Comedy* can be recognized.

Finally, although my book has humor, it is not a spoof of the *Divine Comedy*. Rather, it is a fictional revision which adds modern science and theology to an old classic.

The Inferno 2.0

Canto 1

Introduction, meeting Dante

Half-way through a normal human lifespan
I found myself lost within a desert
which looked like it had once been a forest.

There were stumps of mighty ancient trees which,
as far as my eye could see, had been logged
by many generations of woodsmen.

Between the tree stumps, gasping to survive
with desperate roots reaching for moisture,
were stunted weeds and mutated saplings.

How I journeyed there, I cannot recall.
perhaps a blackout following a binge.
At any rate I could not see a path.

But in the distance a mountain arose,
so huge it hoarded all the sunlight
and left my desolate plain dimly lit.

With little daylight left I hiked toward
that mount, which seemed the only logical
place where I could hope for timely rescue.

The rocky ground rose slightly as I walked,
first with boulders growing ever larger,
then with treacherous rocky outcroppings.

I longed to reach the mountaintop to rest
but weariness prevented my ascent.
I looked behind me to check my progress

when, shocked, I saw the path I had traversed
was now a trench surrounded by barbed wire
and I was in the midst of World War I!

So, terrified, I leaped back to my feet
and nearly backed into the tusks of a
mastodon (which I thought had been extinct).

Reeling around, a flock of Passenger
Pigeons battered my flailing arms and head
and pushed me into yet more dead species.

I ran back to the trench, despite my fear
of what new surreal horror would await,
when suddenly a cloaked human appeared.

I cried out, "Help me! Get me out of here!
Where am I? Who are you? Why are we here?"
The man stood motionless at first, then said,

"My name was Dante Alighieri.
Just as the poet Virgil was my guide
so now my turn has come to mentor you."

Then, recalling epic poetry,
I stood and stared rudely - my mouth agape.
My denial vanished. I slurred, "Uh – oh."

"Yup," he answered. "We're going on a trip.
Your mother, who still goes to church, has prayed
with tear-stained eyes for your immortal soul."

A string of epithets escaped my tongue
and, horrified, I covered up my mouth.
"There will be plenty time for that," he smirked.

A sickness overtook my mortal gut
as I looked all around, then studied him
who, hopefully, was simply a bad dream.

"No such luck," he said, guessing my sad thoughts.
"For what it's worth," he added, "I too felt
that self-same dread when I first met Virgil."

I answered Dante with a shaking voice,
"So then you'll guide me through the rings of Hell,
then Purgatory up to Paradise?"

"Not quite," he answered. "Things have changed a bit.
With overpopulation Hell is full.
The ancient Hell is covered over now

"and many new Hells had to be produced.
The first prototype is here around us.
The trenches from that War were not enough

"so all those holes left by atomic tests
have been an interim replacement.
Several radioactive craters

"left by Russians and Americans
will probably contain the evil dead."
Then as an afterthought he said, "For now."

He took my arm and said, "Here, take my cloak.
It's rated to protect your mortal flesh
from alpha, beta, gamma and x-rays."

Then, urging me along he said, "Let's go"
"No, wait!" I cried. "Those animals ahead
will tear me limb from limb or eat me whole!"

Then Dante shook his head and answered me,
"They're all extinct, remember? Humankind
destroyed them all therefore they don't exist."

So fearfully I followed Dante's lead.
We wandered past those hollow-eyed skulls which
had witnessed new atrocities of war.

We hiked again back to the barren plain
and saw, from stumps, how massive trees once were.
Those fearsome beasts were fading now from view

and I felt guilty that they were extinct.
Then, struggling to recall my Classic Lit
I turned to ask my Mentor and my Guide,

"If I recall correctly our first place
will be a gate to Hell that has a sign,
'Abandon all hope Ye who enter here'."

"Oh, really," he replied, rolling his eyes.
"I guess if you unsophisticated
types need cheap clichés then it will be so."

"But actually," the sage continued,
"don't you think that back on Earth there are those
already enduring a hopeless hell

"while small percentages of people live
as if there were no need to share God's Grace?
There is no need to specify a place

"uniquely meant for misery and pain."
"No disrespect intended," I replied,
"But haven't things improved since you were here?"

"Far from starvation," I continued on,
"It seems like everyone is now obese.
And people live much longer than before.

"And look at our inventions —certainly
you would have liked our indoor plumbing and
electric lights and planes and telephones..."

He answered, "As we go along our way
you'll see what I've observed for centuries
of progress, best intentions and ideas.

"The twentieth century saw the birth
of technical, creative, shiny new
sins, debauch, cruelty and novel vice."

We kept along our way as he explained,
"So the Hells had to be reorganized -
not just expanded to hold more sinners."

"How so?" I asked, and struggled to keep up.
He answered, "There will be time for questions
later on. For now time is running short.

"Good Friday was the day," said Dante, "that
my own enlightenment journey began.
It's early afternoon now. Let's hurry.

"You'll probably feel the Earth rumbling soon."

Canto II

denial, Dante explains the itinerary, the elevator

A sudden wave of doubt and fear seized me.
"Wait, Dante!" helplessly I cried to him,
"Since this must be some sort of lucid dream

"I must insist on waiting to wake up
or else wait 'til whatever drug I took
wears off sufficiently to think again.

"No need for me to experience a
nightmare, whether sleep- or drug-induced.
After all, my meditation lessons,

"and my reading, and my studies, and my
different therapists have taught me to
avoid all negative or bad thinking..."

"Oh, shut up and follow me!" barked Dante.
"I'm not too fond of travelling through Hell
again myself. And Purgatory's not

"my favorite location either. Just
be grateful for a second chance, you nerd!
Not everyone has prayers said for them."

Then walking onward he muttered something
about "stupid tourists", "ungrateful bums"
and "why can't someone else save these morons?"

"Forgive me, Dante!" I shouted to the
back of his head because he was hiking
far ahead of me and gaining more ground.

"Don't leave me here! I'll pay attention to
everything you say and try to explain!"
The land ahead looked worse than that behind.

The Poet only slowed his pace enough
for me to close the distance between us.
"It's just that I don't understand," I whined.

"I mean, I'm not Aeneas or Saint Paul.
You, too," I added, "wrote about your doubts.
Except you said it much more fluently."

At last my Guide paused, turned, and with a sigh
said, "I'm sorry, too. I've done this route so
many times that I, too, am speaking in

"your crude vernacular. Sometimes I wish
that I was guiding Sartre again. Or Pope
or Nietzsche or someone who is smart."

Then, studying my face he said at last,
"OK then. Here's the itinerary.
First we'll briefly stop to talk to Virgil.

"Try to keep your mouth shut. He is still a
specialist in eloquent spoken and
written language. I hope I don't forget

"my years of education and discourse
because I had to dummy down for you.
Then we'll take a more familiar route

"At least you read or heard about my work.
Some of you dolts don't even know enough
to understand how many things have changed."

We walked awhile in silence on a path
that, unlike common folklore, wasn't wide
or easy or paved with good intentions.

In fact, judging by its difficulty,
it seemed like people really have to work
to earn their treasured place in Perdition.

Perhaps the brambles, underbrush and thorns
that guard the path are embellishments for
hangovers and venereal disease

that people must enjoy in order to
pursue their lives of sin. "We're almost here,"
said Dante. "Wait here. I will be right back."

Then I watched him saunter to another
gentleman, who probably was Virgil.
They greeted each other with fist bumps

then they took out a scroll and studied it.
Pointing first to the scroll and then to some
areas around us they shrugged, studied

the scroll again, pointed, and finally
Dante returned. "Sorry," he said. "We have
some road construction. Typical for Hell."

A short trek later we were standing in
front of a pair of elevator doors.
Dante sort of had to push me inside.

"It's only Hell," he said. "And you have a
round-trip ticket. Relax." There were hundreds
of buttons for floors on the side panel.

Soon we were hearing moans and screams outside.
Ignoring them my Guide began to speak.
"Hell's divided into three main levels.

"The lowest is the level of 'The Hells
We Wish For Others'. Then the next level
is 'The Hells We Choose For Ourselves.' The third

"level is 'The Hell of Reality'.
It is the uppermost level and yet
it is the oldest and most brutal.

"Each level is subdivided into
more specific retraining areas,
depending on the nature of one's sin."

"What do you mean by 'retraining'?" I asked.
The elevator passed more screams and groans.
"The human will," said Dante, "is more free

"than most of us believe is possible.
The souls you'll meet have chosen to be here,
which makes their punishment the more severe."

"Why would a person choose to go to Hell?"
I asked in shock amid the muffled cries.
"The human spirit is a fickle thing."

said Dante. We continued our descent.
My Guide then shook his head and gave a shrug.
"Every incarnation we work through

"we have specific lessons we must learn.
Sometimes we pass the course - sometimes we fail
and have to be reborn to learn again.

"And there are others who abuse the rules
so badly that they may not be reborn
until the lessons they were sent to learn

"are treated more respectfully. That's when
the spirit is allowed to choose again
whether to stay in Hell or be reborn.

"For some, the choice is to remain in Hell.
The incarnation on our planet Earth
is one of the toughest places to learn.

"But Earth is also one of the quickest
places in the multiverse to learn and
grow toward spiritual maturity.

"Despite the suffering of those below,
sometimes the familiarity of
Hell is easier for souls to handle."

The elevator shuddered to a halt.

Canto III

admissions line, the nature of Satan

The noise, no longer buffered by the doors,
was a cacophony of ghostly shrieks,
wails, motorcycle engines, whips and chains.

Incredulous, I muttered to myself,
"motorcycles?..." Dante said, "They need those
to herd the newest souls to their placements."

"That club on Earth was such a good idea
that it was borrowed here below. Nice touch,
hey? These bikers are genuine Hell's Angels.

"They also liked 'Ghost Riders in the Sky'."
I looked around. That famous sign was gone,
but there were arrows, traffic signs and ropes

like one would see in any lengthy queue.
A single soul sprinted to escape and
a dozen bikers with wings chased him down.

The beatings drew attention for awhile
then the other souls moved ahead in line,
replaced by multitudes of newcomers.

A single clerk created bottlenecks
as he checked each ID and pointed where
that soul was to report, then hollered, "Next!"

Hell's bikers kept the line of souls controlled
with whips and chains if anyone spoke out,
while that lone clerk, ignoring all the noise

kept calling for ID's and yelling, "Next!"
Once past his desk a soul would disappear
as if it had vaporized in a flash.

"That's the Admissions Line," stated Dante.
"I've known of souls who had to stay in line
for years before they got their assignment.

I looked around, astonished, then I said,
"After that long elevator ride we
must be at the bottom levels of Hell."

"We are indeed," my Master gave reply.
I gazed at him and said, "But in your book
you started at the top and worked your way

"down to the feet of Satan. Then you crawled
with Virgil past His toes and into light,
escaping into Purgatory. So

"where's Satan?" I looked carefully around.
A backward glance at me and then he teased,
"Why? Is He expecting you or something?"

The wailing sobs of souls and roaring bikes
put me into a humorless mindset.
Dante saw my dour mood and uttered,

"Relax…" I snapped back at him, "Yeah, I know.
It's only Hell. Where's Satan? I was right.
this whole thing really is just a bad dream!"

Sighing, he took my arm and led me past
the entry gate. The clerk knew better than
complain about our cutting in the line.

"There is no Satan," Dante said at last.
We stepped around some body parts and gore.
"You're kidding me!" I exclaimed. "He's spoken

"of in one form or another by all
the world's religions! Even atheists
seem to believe in the Fallen Angel.

"You do know who I'm talking about, right?"
"Of course I do!" the Poet snapped at me.
"I thought you said you read the *Comedy*."

I shook my head and muttered, "I don't get
any of these horrible happenings.
How do I get out of here? I've had it!"

Then Dante laughed and guided me around
a pile of steaming volcanic rocks.
"Be patient. The answers will come in time.

"For now you'll have to trust me," Dante said.
"And I apologize for teasing you.
It's just that some concepts are challenging."

He kicked a skull aside and stepped around
another mound of decomposing bones.
"I'll do my best to teach. You try to learn."

I said sarcastically, "So then there is
no such thing as Evil or suffering.
Cruelty and injustice aren't real."

"Something like that," he said, moving along.
"Our consciousness is one of the forces
of nature, like motion and energy.

"The thing you call Satan is a thought-form,
created by many generations
of angry, hurt or otherwise betrayed

"beings who, not disciplining products
of their minds, unleashed the greatest evils
in space-time." The Poet paused for awhile.

    "It's hard for people to believe the might
of their own words and thoughts," the Poet said.
"The self-restraint and discipline that's taught

"in all the religions' holy books
is vital to contain the wickedness
that intellects are able to conjure.

"Oh, by the way," Dante added, "you're right.
We are starting at the bottom of Hell
and working our way up. Things are awry

"with all of this reorganization.
Now, where was I? Oh yes. The nature of
Evil…" I shook my head and said, "Hold on!"

"If all of this is true then why did you
Write your *Divine Comedy* as you did?
You wrote that Hell has nine separate rings

"and the worst sinners are at the bottom -
your philosophy's consistent with the
classical theologies and dogmas."

Dante shrugged casually and replied,
"Galileo gave in to the Church, too.
Those guys in Rome weren't always nice, you know."

"So I've read," I answered. "I believe you.
But now another question comes to mind —
if Satan isn't real, then how 'bout God?"

"Oh... Let's not go there yet," was his reply.

Canto IV

why Dante is there, the nature of Evil, Cerberus

We climbed a steep and rocky path within
the type of land the Poet once described.
A question bothered me, though, as we walked.

"Hey, Dante?" I asked him at last. I hoped
I wasn't being tactless when I asked,
"Is that the reason why you have to lead

"this journey through the afterlife?" He stopped.
"What do you mean?" he asked, irritated.
I stammered trying hard to find the words.

"Well... you were led through Hell and Paradise
and all of that for some specific reason.
Was God mad at you because you wrote an

"altered version of what you really saw?"
At first I thought he'd hit me but instead
he muttered softly, "Yeah. Something like that.

"You'll see soon how judgements are decided
which we have earned through our misdeeds and sins.
For now let's concentrate on what's ahead."

We walked a treacherous path until we
reached a castle with a forbidding door.
I exclaimed, and almost shouted out,

"Wait! I remember from the *Comedy*
that Limbo was the first place Virgil showed.
And he was sad because that's where he lived.

"It was the place where virtuous heathens
and unbaptized children were sent to dwell.
They were guiltless but not blessed with God's grace,

"because they hadn't been baptized in Christ."
Dante nodded thoughtfully and asked,
"Does that seem fair to you? Or Godlike?"

His question struck me deep within my soul.
"Uh, why no," I stuttered, "but God doesn't…
do that sort of thing without a reason."

"Or maybe," Dante smiled, "God just doesn't
do that sort of thing at all. To send a
soul to eternal unhappiness and

"torment simply for lack of the right
ritual seems rather petty to me."
I said, "But in the Bible it's written

"'…who believes and is baptized shall be saved.'
You have to believe in Jesus and you
have to be baptized or you'll be damned!"

And Dante answered, "The Muslims believe
that you must believe in Allah or else.
Other religions don't even mention

"exclusive rights to other people's souls.
Perhaps God is bigger that all of that."
"But Jesus said," I protested, "that 'I

"...'am the Way the Truth and the Light. No one
comes to the Father but through me.' " Dante
smiled and said, "Jesus is a torchbearer,

"for those born and raised in Christian countries.
At death most souls need a torchbearer to
follow so that they don't get lost in the

"afterlife. But enough of this. Let's go."
He kept walking ahead and, reluctant
to follow I asked, "Why is there Evil?"

"Evil is easier than doing good.
Our 'lizard brains' do things the easy way
and also possess our basic instincts.

"Hunger, sex, aggression keep us alive
and continue the species, therefore they
in themselves are not a type of Evil.

"However, when these instincts harm others,
then rape, murder, violence, theft and such
are criminal acts, not survival skills.

"With acceptance of a higher Thought-Form
into our hearts we strive to control these
basic drives and use them constructively."

"But why..." I began, but Dante journeyed
onward. "So many questions," he replied,
"and we still haven't begun our study."

"I've actually seen enough," I said.
He laughed a most undignified guffaw,
that rang in sharp contrast to others' wails.

"Dude, you ain't seen nothin' yet!" he chuckled.
"Remember, we are starting out," he browsed
his map, "by visiting the 'Hells We Wish

"On Others'. The first partition of that
area is for tyrants, sadistic
bullies and the people who revere them."

The dark foreboding castle loomed ahead,
made worse by a cloudy, threatening sky
and lightning bolts partnered by thunder claps.

As we drew nearer to the castle door
and crossed Leviathan-infested moats,
Cerberus stepped aside to let us in.

"Don't pet it!" Dante snapped. "Just because it
didn't take your arm off doesn't mean it
always tolerates idiots like you!"

I snapped by hand back and heard a low growl
from one or two of the heads on the beast.
"Good dog," I whispered. Dante didn't hear.

Once inside, the screams and shouts and groans
grew louder. We walked briskly down a hall.
A dungeon-like environment deepened

the sounds of human misery so much
that footsteps echoing on cobblestones
were too faint to be heard, as were our words.

Therefore, in silence I followed Dante.

Canto V

the castle of the tyrants

My Master led me down a corridor
with door-like windows lining either side
like in a prison's solitary block.

He motioned me ahead, and opening
a heavy window-door, the cries within
grew louder. Still, he made me look inside.

A man who had a tiny brush mustache
and a bad haircut was tied to a cross.
He was surrounded by adoring fans.

They numbered in the multitudes and though
their faces bore exhaustion and defeat
they held their right arms high and cried to him,

"Hail Victory!" without a pause for breath.
A winged being poked anyone who tried
to lower his arm or rest his hoarse throat.

"There were many more like him," Dante said,
"but none were quite as famous as this guy."
The Poet watched awhile and said at last,

"You can speak to anybody you wish
if you can tear them away from their zeal.
The crucified one in the middle might

"like to explain why he doesn't want to
repent and go to Purgatory yet."
Surprised, I looked askance then did as told.

"See how they love me!" was the man's reply.
And so I asked a follower the same.
"See how he loves me!" was the fan's reply.

"In fact I'll even die and kill for him."
And almost like an echo the man said,
"In fact they'll even die and kill for me."

Shaking his head, the Poet said, "They all
know they have the power to leave at will,
and begin to heal in Purgatory."

Then we closed the window and moved along.
Dante opened a different window.
This one had Nero with a laurel wreath

and toga standing in a boiling pot
surrounded by beginning fiddlers
who also were boiled in their own cauldrons.

"You there!" yelled Dante to a violin
student who was grinding out a B-flat.
"Why don't you go where Redemption is?"

With glowing smile the student answered us,
"I've never played the violin before
and he said I can play while cities burn!"

The Master asked the boiling man, "And you!
You know that you can leave if you just vow
to repent the old ways and learn the new."

Not missing any beats the man replied,
"But who, then, will be left to teach these ones
the way to fiddle while a city burns?"

Cautiously I said, "That's not logical."
"You're right," Dante replied, "but then down here
it doesn't have to be." We closed the door.

"How many dungeons like this one exist?"
I asked as we came to the next one. "As
many as we need. Here, look in this one."

Shocked, I watched as Joseph Stalin was cut
into about twenty million pieces
and made into a soup with his own blood.

hen slowly Stalin emerged to re-form
himself, and once again the meat grinder
made him into another soup with blood.

This happened and kept happening again
slowly enough so that, while whole, Stalin
could answer questions from Dante and me.

Responding to the questions asked before,
"Can't you see that I'm in complete control?
And I have all the power in the world!"

"But Premier Stalin," I protested to
the soup, "you were not even feeding your
own people!" The dissolving Stalin said

with scorn, "The people can go feed themselves."
He said no more as he cooked in the pot.
I saw that Pol Pot had his own dungeon.

The twentieth century dictators
seemed to monopolize that part of Hell,
although the ancients had some holdovers.

Dante explained that Attila the Hun
repented, and now contemporary
scholars study the Hun's management skills.

Then I saw a stairway with a large door.
"We're not allowed to go there," Dante said.
"Otherwise we will disturb their studies."

My curiosity was piqued. I asked,
"Who is there and what are they studying?"
"In classrooms taught by volunteers," he said

"numerous petty tyrants, warlords, a
bunch of kings, some CEO's and corrupt
politicians are sent to their classrooms

"where they study Empathy 101
and have boring seminars on niceness.
Also Remedial Morality.

"Some have a lab course on 'How Torture Feels'
which is taught by victims of their torture.
So far none of them have passed their exams."

"I can't believe these villains have a chance
at Heaven," I complained. The Poet was
serene when he answered, "It's not without

"genuine remorse, desire for change and
willingness to undo their Karma in
Purgatory. That can take centuries.

"Some true psychopaths are so damaged that
their souls have to be demolished in that
lake of Fire you may have read about.

"And some just choose to rot in misery."
He shrugged and shook his head in wonderment.
He said after awhile, "To each his own.

"That is the nature of free human will."

Canto VI

violent zealots

We climbed the steps past classrooms of the damned
and once again a soul tried to escape.
The Hounds of Hell chased him down and dragged him,

back to his dungeon classroom full of pain.
For some reason, unbeknownst to me, my
memory flashed back to Calculus class.

On exiting the castle into air
that was as dark and dank as that inside
my foot squished into something wiggling, gross

and utterly revolting. Looking down
I saw in horror it was a body part.
It seemed to be a forearm with a hand.

I didn't realize I'd screamed out loud
until Dante touched my shoulder gently.
"Just watch your step," he said, reassuring.

"I realize this must be difficult
for someone who is not used to such gore.
You'll see a lot of body parts that try

"to reattach themselves where they belonged
until a suicide bomb scattered them
around, as you see here. Oops! Watch that foot!"

I managed to avoid that groping foot
that seemed to crawl in search of someone's leg.
I also side-stepped a head that cried out,

"Allahu Akbar!" as it rolled around
searching for a spinal column and neck.
I started to query that severed head

But then I almost stepped on a liver
which was attaching itself to a heart,
except the heart was already taken.

"You may have guessed," said Dante, "that this is
the place where over-zealots of all creeds
come when using violence to convert

"others to their unique way of thinking.
The Cossacks of Catherine the Great are
over yonder," he said, pointing to a cliff.

"Just as they forced the Russian peasantry
to be baptized to an unfamiliar faith,
so they must ride their horses past the brink.

"And over there," he pointed to a spit,
"are priests who tortured women to confess
to being witches, so they could be burned."

Then over to the left I saw two groups
of souls who grappled for one narrow plank
that teetered over a bottomless pit.

"Those are Hindus and the others Muslims.
They died in India while trying to
convert each other to the other's faith.

"Beyond those plains are many other groups
who slaughtered and destroyed the cultures of
potential converts, whether the converts

"chose it or not. These souls are some of the
most difficult to save. They all believe
too strongly that they must evangelize.

"It's hard to teach them how important it
is to respect the will of others as
much as our Creator reveres our own."

I argued with that. "The Bible says we
must go forth and spread the Gospel over
all the Earth, baptizing them in the name

"of the Father, Son and the Holy Ghost.
How am I supposed to reconcile what
I was taught with what you're teaching me now?"

Dante nodded. "The Bible also says,
'when ye go forth, be wise as serpents but
harmless as doves.' Doves to not terrorize.

"Saint Paul also says that we are to go
forth and teach the Word, and if our teachings
are rejected, wish them well and move on.

"Nowhere are we commanded to convert
others by force, neither in the Bible
nor the Koran nor any other Book.

"Many sins come from interpreting the
letter of the law to reflect our own
bigotries and desires. The Bible

"is often quoted out of context, I'm
sure you hear that a lot, and Christians who
do so are sometimes called 'Cafeteria

"Christians' because they take a verse they do
like and ignore the verses they don't like.
On the other hand the spirit of the

"law is that once we hear the word and are
transformed by it for the better, we share
our joy and commitment with others so

"that they, too, can have a chance to renew
their tired and searching souls as we have.
But this is too passive for some people,

"and teaching by example is the most
difficult way to teach, although it is
the most effective. It requires us

"to actually live the commandments
and not just lecture on them. The Greatest
Commandment – to love God and then to love

"others as much as ourselves – is
a really tricky one. Some people can't
love themselves, some people can't love others.

"But you'll see more of that as we go on."

Canto VII

prophesy, Dante offers to cancel the Journey

"Dante, why do I have to do this?" I
wept. Tears flowed down my cheeks as I told him,
"These visions you're showing me are too much!"

"I'm afraid I'll go insane if I have
to witness much more. Or maybe I am
already." Placing a kind hand on my

shoulder, Dante said gently, "'Blessed are
those who hunger and thirst for righteousness,
for they shall be satisfied.' You've always

"been a seeker, haven't you?" I choked down
a sob and nodded. "You are going through
the agony of Faust, who sold his soul

"for knowledge. Yours is the supposed sin
of Adam and Eve who ate of the Tree
Of Knowledge. One can no longer bask in

"ignorance after beginning the Great
Journey. This Journey is labelled sinful and
heretical because it is as

"frightening to those who watch us travel
it as it is for ourselves. Take heart," he said,
the Journey, too, is something we do not

"have to take, just like with these souls you've seen.
The temptation to remain childlike
and let others think for us is strong.

"Those who have prayed for you are those who were
frightened by the changes the Quest creates.
But for us it just meant you were ready."

A quick shoulder hug, then he asked, "You are,
aren't you?" I pulled away a bit and said,
"My training says this could be demonic

"deception. Satan tries every ruse to
win our souls..." Dante nodded. "As I said,
you can stop this Great Journey if you'd like."

I eyed him suspiciously and said, "You
mean I can postpone it until later..."
He stared at me intently. "Let me call

"the angels and send you home." "No, wait," I
exclaimed, "I guess I just needed to rest.
I'm sorry I was so rude. Where to next?"

He looked me over carefully. "We're still
in the Violent Crimes area. The
shades you'll see used sexual violence."

"Will it hurt?" "No. They're all restrained." "Will they
say nasty things to us?" "Maybe" "Will there
be any more gore or torture?" "Not here."

"Hey, Dante?" I asked timidly. "What now?"
He answered briskly, as if waiting for
me to ask him for a loan or something.

"In the *Comedy* you wrote that the shades
could foretell the future. Is that the truth?"
Seeming to relax a bit he said, "Yes."

Turning to a writhing spirit nearby
I asked, "Do you know which team will win the
Superbowl this year?" Dante glared at me.

With a voice quavering in agony
the spirit replied, "How can you ask such
a stupid question when the world teeters

"on collapse?! I'll tell you of a future
event! New York City will be attacked
by a group called Al Qaeda. Thousands will

"die and Iraq will be plunged into war!"
"Again?!" I exclaimed. The spirit, puzzled,
shrugged and asked, "What do you mean by 'again'?"

I answered tactfully, "That already
happened in 2001." Sitting bolt
upright from the muck the spirit lay in

he asked, "What do you mean by 2001?
Isn't it 1877?"
I struggled to contain a mocking laugh.

"That was over a century ago."
Defensive, he said, "OK, so I don't
get out much!" He plopped back into the muck.

Bubbling up from the mud-pit came the words,
"I prophesied that right, though, didn't I!"
"OK, that's enough you two!" Dante said

angrily. "We have a lot of ground to
cover yet and we do have a timeframe."
We walked along quietly for awhile,

passing one or two unremarkable
spirits. I was becoming more attuned
to my surroundings by then. Finally

we reached a dried-up riverbed with a
sign that read, "River Styx. Contact Charon."
Dante reached again for his map and gazed

ahead. "We'll have to take this detour." He
pointed to a narrow mountain pass
that led upward to a suspension bridge.

"If you look carefully," he pointed to
the distant shore on the other side of the
bridge, "you might catch sight of the Cherubim."

Straining my eyes I glimpsed flying angels.

Canto VIII

child abusers

We came upon a bridge that looked as if
it hadn't been maintained for centuries,
with missing planks and fraying ropes that held

the bridge aloft. There wasn't any breeze
but yet it swayed intimidatingly.
Even Dante hesitated to cross.

Beneath us gaped a mountainous chasm
with sharp forbidding rocks to fall upon.
And far below along a distant shore

sat a very pissed-off boatman with his
empty ferry. Dante grumbled under
his breath, "Get over it, Charon." Stepping

gingerly along the wooden planks I
almost fell through a rotten board that gave
way. Before I had a chance to cry for

help, two Cherubim appeared and grasped my
arms, whisking me across to the other side.
Dante thanked them and accepted something

from one of them, then slipped it in his robe.
"You who are still alive are heavy," he said.
"The boatmen, too, get mad when they capsize."

A faint pungent aroma, like sewage,
then filled my nostrils. "Here," Dante said, "take
this handkerchief that the angel gave me.

"It will help you breathe more easily." It
was a plain white kerchief with a pleasant
scent. "This region can get quite ripe at times."

Rounding a bend the stench almost knocked me
over. The handkerchief proved a godsend,
so to speak. The land ahead of us was

brightly colored, yet filthy with feces
and other excreta. There appeared to
be plastic children's blocks in primary

colors, locked together with holes peeking
through the vast surface. Stuck inside the holes
were spirits helplessly writhing in place

to avoid the adorable naked
Cherubs, like the ones who met us at the
bridge. In multitudes they giggled and flew

above the trapped unfortunates below.
Like well-fed pigeons hovering aloft,
they released their intestinal contents

on the groaning wraiths below them with glee.
I asked my Guide who these poor sinners were
who were helplessly drenched in baby poop.

"These are the child molesters," he replied.
"In life they preyed on helpless innocents.
They couldn't stay away from kids so now

"they get to watch as many naked butts
as they'd want flying overhead to pee.
These dudes are generally quickest to

"repent and beg for Purgatory, but
public opinion keeps them here longer
than most. Watch your head!" A Cherub with bad

aim nearly missed me and deposited a
mass of salmonella-smelling poop so
close it almost contaminated me.

"Sorry!" the little angel giggled as
it fluttered away like a butterfly.
"If you've seen enough," said Dante, wiping his

sleeve with a disgusted grimace on his
face. "In fact even if you haven't seen
enough, let's get out of here. The next place

"is a bit different but is on a
similar vein. It's the area of
rapists, seducers, perverts

"and general low-lives who didn't quite
get the message about using sex as
an expression of adult tenderness."

We hiked up to a settlement that looked
like some sort of gated community.
Standing in front of the gate were some guards.

They were nasty-looking with spears, shields and
togas plus leather limb guards, like Roman
centurions. At their sides were short swords.

They had plumed helmets like the Romans wore.
As we approached, the guards snapped into a
formation, spears ready, shields raised aloft.

"Looks like the perverts lawyered up again,"
Dante muttered in disgust. I remarked,
"Those are lawyers?" He nodded. "Where did they

"come from?" I asked again. Dante rolled his
eyes and said, "This is Hell. Where do you think?"
Turning to the guards he yelled, "Let us in!"

The response from the leader was, "Sorry.
According to Section forty, Part C
subsection two zero nine eight point five

"of the Codex no one who is alive
may enter said facility without…"
"Move it or I'll sic some angels on you!"

As quickly as the centurions formed
up they broke rank and permitted us to
enter. "You've done this before, haven't you!"

I told my Master in admiration.
He nodded, silent, and urged me forward.
Some centurions leered, some turned away

and we reached the doorway without further
challenges. Dante asked me abruptly,
"Are you afraid of snakes?" Taken aback

I responded, "I'm not too fond of them…"
"Well, try to keep your revulsion under
control," he said. He reached behind a door.

Then Dante handed me a cattle prod.

Canto IX

the sexually violent

Once inside the portal of those damned souls
we blinked against the absolute darkness,
hearing only slithering sounds and moans.

I grabbed Dante's arm, afraid again,
as I had already done many times.
Beneath his reassuring touch I felt

him reach for something. Then a torch was lit.
"Turn out that damned light!" screamed a snake beneath
us. Or at least I thought it was a snake.

Larger than a python with a human
head, an ugly face glared at us and coiled
its body into a quivering knot.

"I said turn it off!" And the creature was
joined in this complaint by others of its
species, as far as the torchlight could shine.

"Be quiet!!" Dante shouted back. Then he
turned to me, explaining, "Those are the souls
who cherished darkness while committing

"their crimes of sexual predation. Now
their limbs, which raped and beat sadistically,
and their genitals which they mistreated

"are encased in the bodies of serpents
so that they cannot use them to exploit
others again. It also teaches them

"what helplessness feels like when aggressors
steal their peace and violate their bodies."
I recoiled at the sight of all those

writhing snakes, struggling to avoid the light.
"But why," I asked, "are they so afraid of
light?" Brandishing the torch at one of them

who was trying to crawl up my legs he
snapped, "Use the cattle prod! Don't let any
of them get that close to you! Mercy on

"sinners does not mean allowing them to
sin against you." I pushed the prod into
another human-headed snake who screamed

at the pain I inflicted. Right away
I apologized, and Dante scolded
me, "Why are you empowering these scum?"

"I'm sorry," this time reflexively I
said to Dante. He scolded me again,
"Stop apologizing for protecting

"your own space. Part of the challenge of this
realm is respecting yourself enough to
fight for your personal autonomy

"as much as you are able. Some victims
of these brutes cannot fight successfully
against their attackers. Then the duty

"of the victim is to find the strength to
believe once again in their rights and fight
to carry on. These vermin you see are

"afraid of light because it forces them
to see who they really are." I prodded
another creature and this time when it

yelped I ignored it. "That's better," Dante
said approvingly. Then turning to a snake
he asked, "Why don't you get out of this pit

"and beg for the restructuring of your
soul in Purgatory?" The snake slithered
away from the torch and hissed, "They'll take

"away my memories of all those young
girls who were asking for it and then cried
afterwards just to cover their own lust."

"You're right, Dante," I said and then I zapped
the creature with the cattle prod a few
times just for the hell of it, so to speak.

Dante didn't respond. He stepped forward
along an eroded path, which was cleared
reluctantly by resentful serpents.

The darkness grew less pervasive as we
carefully made our way through the snake pit.
I slipped a couple times and was met with

some angry hiss as the Master Dante
grabbed my collar and pulled me back onto
the treacherous path. After awhile the

darkness retreated enough so that I
wasn't as dependent on the hazy
torchlight to find my way along the path.

Thankfully, the snake pit was behind us.
Dante chuckled a bit as he said, "You
can set down the cattle prod now. And the

"handkerchief you received from the Cherub."
"I'm afraid to let go of them," I said
hesitantly. My Guide smiled a bit and

responded, "You'll get all the tools you need
as we journey along. This is that 'Faith'
thing you keep hearing about." "But what if..."

I started to say. He reached abruptly
for a rocky outcropping, grabbing it
with both hands while swinging himself under.

I did the same, following him. Ahead
was a rugged path leading upward through
a mountain pass that limited our view.

Panting, I followed his quick mountain-goat
steps up the trail, around another bend,
and onto a plateau where we rested.

"Those Violent Against Nature is next."

Canto X

those Violent Against Nature

"Enough rest. We have a long way to go
yet," Dante said cheerfully. I just groaned
and got up barely in time to follow.

I asked the back of his head, "You said the
next area is about violence
to nature or something?" I wasn't sure

if he was eager to move on or if
he was eager to leave the previous
areas. "Yes," he replied, not breathless

as we climbed a steep cliff. "Slow down!" I yelled.
"Unlike you I still need to use lungs and
stuff for breathing!" He paused and looked back at

me. "Sorry. This next realm is a recent
enhancement. It is for polluters and
others who damaged that part of the Earth

"that was entrusted to their stewardship."
He gave me a hand and pulled me over
the top of a plateau. "In it we have

"a modern nobility cross-section:
CEO's of energy companies,
lumber barons, chemical industry

"executives, a few generals who
liked to strip their battlefields bare, and of
course lots of politicians who traded

"land rights for votes. There's real estate moguls
who auctioned off so much of our coastlines
and the people who bought those properties.

"I can't forget to mention hunters and
habitat thieves who exterminated
many species in various epochs."

He almost seemed gleeful as we travelled.
"There are air and water polluters, strip
miners, resource abusers. Here we are."

I looked over a massive bubbling tar
pit with thousands of souls boiling within.
"We'll have to use the walkway," said Dante.

This bridge was another precarious
walkway with rotting timbers and frayed ropes.
"Don't be scared," Dante said. "If you kept up

"with recycling and using Earth-friendly
products you don't have to worry about
falling in." Shaking, I whispered, "Oh, God."

"God's not here right now," Dante countered. "We're
in Hell, remember?" "How could I forget!?"
He laughed and said, "Here, jump on my back. You'll

"be safe if I carry you across." I
wasn't sure how a dead poet would be
able to carry my mortal weight, but

I piggy-backed onto him anyway.
His body was surprisingly solid.
"Don't get too comfortable," he warned me.

"I can only do this for a short while."
It was long enough for a dead soul to
holler out from the pit, "You there! Get me

"out of here!" Not skipping a beat Dante
said, "You know the rules. You stay here until
that mess you created on Earth is cleaned

"up." As we quickly passed him by he yelled,
"But that will take centuries!" The spirit's
voice faded into the distance. We were

already on the solid face of the
other shore, but we could still hear a few
voices offering us substantial bribes.

I thanked my Guide profusely as he sat
me down. "You're welcome." I reached over to
grasp him in a hug and my arms fell through.

Appearing not to notice my blunder
Dante said cheerfully, "Let's visit some
swindlers, con-artists, thieves and other crooks."

We came up to what looked like computer
chips, except they were massive and had eyes.
"This is another recent addition.

"It's the Technologically Fraudulent."
I surveyed another kingdom that seemed
to stretch for miles. Many of the chips seemed

lifeless because they had no way to see.
I inquired about this and Dante said,
"This region is growing so fast we had

"to build ahead. Here we have computer
scam artists, hackers, computer vandals
who can destroy brick-and-mortar online.

"There are cyber bullies, lazy system
operators whose lack of diligence
caused a lot of suffering for people

"who didn't do anything wrong except
become dependent on computers for
their everyday needs, like everyone else."

He looked around. "You can't see them from here,
but there are some older technologies
off in the distance. Most inventions, for

"example, were reconfigured to wage
war, medical discoveries were used
only for people who could afford them.

"Even the printing press and other mass
media were abused for purposes
of spreading propaganda. You yourself

"alluded to this intellectual
pollution when we first met. Such a waste
of creative potential is sinful."

He shook his head and said, "Man. If I'd had
the Internet back in my day I could
have published *The Comedy* online and

"avoided the censure..." he suddenly
looked wistful. It took me by surprise to
see him like that, so I remained quiet.

And quietly we went to see some more.

Canto XI

on heresy,

"In the *Divine Comedy*," I started,
"you wrote quite a bit about the torments
given to heretics and suicides…"

"I didn't write that!" he snapped. "My censors
wrote those pieces!" Hesitantly I asked,
"What do you mean — censors?" He almost snarled

in reply, "the medieval Church didn't
like competition so it labelled all
other theologies besides its own

"as heresy and damned all heretics
to eternal hellfire as punishment
for not wholly adopting Church doctrine.

"The more recent European conquests
like Ireland and Scandinavian
lands had their own pagan religions which

"were reinvented as devil worship
by the Church fathers who wanted
more dues-paying converts. Many of these

"pagan lands had natural resources
that helped fatten the treasury in Rome.
That classical image of Satan was

"adapted from Cerunnos, a Celtic
god, who had horns. Most peoples had mother
goddesses and refused to give them up.

"So, Mary was exalted in status.
Also the pagans had their esteemed feast
days and no amount of preaching could tear

"them away from partying mid-winter
and in spring. Therefore, Christmas is the time
when a father-god was born and Easter

"is a beloved spring fertility
festival with bunnies and eggs. The date
of Easter is set each year according

"to the moon's relationship with the spring
equinox — a huge pagan compromise
designed to win over the hearts and minds

"of pagans, because Zoroastrian —
based threats of hellfire only go so far.
You attract more flies with honey than with

"vinegar, as they say. Festivals of
lesser importance were changed to saints' days
because sometimes the peasants just needed

"a day off from work. If a belief or
doctrine wasn't declared heresy, then
it was morphed into a Church holiday."

We climbed a set of rocky stairs which wound
around a cliff. Dante continued to
talk as we climbed. "The heresy concept

"began in the early Church around the
time of Constantine. Christianity
was becoming a force to be reckoned

"with and at the time there were several
different Christian doctrines. One believed
that Christ was fully divine, one believed

"that Christ was something else, another
believed that the way to salvation was
through gnosis, another sect labelled the

"Gnostics as sexual deviants and
so forth. So the Council of Nicaea
was held to unify the Christian church."

We stepped over another pile of bones
that littered our path. "The Council censored
all gospels that didn't fit their final

"compromised canon. What was left was the
New Testament. The other gospels were
burned, and so were some of their adherents."

Far ahead was a laboratory
building. I wanted to ask what it was
but Dante was on a roll. "Just what is

"heresy anyway? he sermonized.
"Are Christians heretics because Muslims
say they are or is it the other way

"around? Isn't any belief that draws
one closer to God divinely inspired?
Wouldn't it be logical for God to

"reveal Itself to different cultures
in ways that each culture can appreciate?"
Struggling to keep up with his discourse I

asked, "Itself?" Dante answered, "Itself or
Himself or Herself, whatever. God does
not have genitalia, last I heard."

I agreed eagerly because some huge
thunderclouds were rolling in, darkening
a sky that was already dull from sin.

"Um, Dante?" I began. "Maybe we should
hurry to get inside that building there."
"Why?" "Because it's looking like rain," I said.

He glanced up and responded, "Pull up your
hood. It's all acid rain plus nuclear
fallout down here. Anyway as I was

"saying, we do not have a circle of
heretics. When censors confiscated
my manuscript they added it themselves."

Stepping up the pace a bit I remarked,
"So part of your great epic was written
by an anonymous cleric?" Looking

back at Dante, I couldn't tell if the
droplet on his cheek was a tear or a
drop of acid rain. He dawdled behind

me a little as the rain began to pour
more heavily. "Written, deleted and
finally lost altogether," he said.

"And their cover story was that I was
exiled from Florence for political
reasons." Hastily I offered him an

apology for his unfortunate
circumstances as I dashed for the door
of the building. Seeming oblivious

to the rain he said, "Actually I
was lucky to escape with my life." Then
looking up he noticed the door and said,

"This is an experimental test site."

Canto XII

the swindlers

Consistent with the laboratory theme,
the place was filled with lab rats, but this time
the rats, wearing scrubs, were running the place.

The rodent lab assistants' jobs were to
provide the nursing care for the subjects
who, with many types of dismemberment,

required oxygen, IV's and Total
Parenteral Nutrition. I surveyed
the room we entered — one of many in

a huge complex. Desensitized by now
to gore and body parts, I saw a few
shades who were missing internal organs.

A few more were also missing limbs and
their torsos plus heads were propped with pillows
so that they could interact with the rats.

Dante explained, "These souls have swindled and
cheated others out of hard-earned money
that was needed to survive. Therefore they

have vital parts removed in proportion
to the living wage they stole from others."
"Hey! Watch where you're stepping!" a body-less

face cried out. I quickly stepped aside and
watched a lab assistant pick up the face
that had plopped onto the floor, then returned

it to the cart from which it had fallen.
After the IV lines were straightened up
Dante asked the face, "So why are you here?"

A rat smoothed out the face enough so it
could speak. "I was an executive in
a large investment firm.

"All I did was leverage loans from bad
credit risks, and for some reason people
claim I ruined the economy for

"personal gain. I just gave investors
what they wanted and got my percentage.
They all signed a statement attesting that

"they understood the risks." A rat in scrubs
interrupted, "The statement was on page
forty-four of a hundred twenty page

"prospectus that was written in a language
even attorneys couldn't understand."
The face replied, "That was not my problem."

Then twisting itself into a grimace
it said to a lab rat, "My nose itches." The
rat obligingly scratched what probably

was, indeed, a nose. Then the face resumed.
"It was not a difficult investment
strategy to understand. They gave me

"their retirement money to invest
and for the most part didn't withdraw it.
When they did want their ten percent return

"I had money from other investors
to cover the loss from my six percent
investments which had decreased in value

"because other investment brokers were
going bankrupt doing the same thing with
their clients. My investors knew the risks."

Dante asked the face, "Don't you feel remorse
for those who had lost their life savings?" "If you
don't understand the rules, don't play the game,"

was the face's reply. The rat reached up
calmly to change the IV solution.
Dante said, "I guess he'll be here awhile."

Many stories came from other torsos
who had lived their lives making easy cash.
A drug dealer whose head floated above

his drug-soaked body exclaimed that he, too,
was a victim because he needed cash
to support his own drug habit. Other

incomplete torsos bragged about lonely
rich widows, but then their rat attendant
cut off their oxygen until the shade

promised to be nice. There were usurers,
insurance frauds, common thieves, computer
hackers, street thugs and televangelists.

There were solicitors for charities,
political causes and home repairs.
In fact, this part of Hell seemed to have

the most diversity of any of
the evil subterranean levels.
As we tried to leave, one spirit tried to

sell Dante a time-share in Florida
and another tried to interest me
in precious metals and collector art.

My Master and I exited with our
pocket change intact and our watches on.
"Do these souls, too, have a chance to redeem

"themselves in Purgatory?" I queried
my Guide. He said, "Only if they agree
to a daily body cavity search."

Emerging outside the lab, we saw that
the rain had stopped. Ahead of us there was
a miles long line of prisoners walking

in a chain gang. Roaring motorcycle
angels kept them moving with whips and chains.
"Those are different kinds of murderers,"

Dante explained. "Spree killers, serial
killers, school shooters, accidental but
unrepentant killers. They're all moving

"to their new renovated location."

Canto XIII

the Hells We Create For Ourselves,
on suicides and hauntings

"We are pretty much out of 'The Hells We
Wish On Others'," said Dante. "Now we move
on to 'The Hells We Create For Ourselves'."

"All these levels of Hell are confusing,"
I said, shaking my head. "That's probably
because they are all in universes

"different from the one we are used to,"
Dante answered. "Huh?" He smiled and replied,
"On Earth each soul develops different

"psychic vibration levels, depending
on how they live their lives and the thoughts they
allow to predominate their spirits."

He held a door open for me and said,
"Are you familiar with the multiverse
concept?" I nodded. "It's confusing, but

"yes, I've heard of it." He said, "That's OK.
Cosmologists, too, are working on it.
Anyway, you already know about the

"electrical activity the brain
generates in the form of brain waves, right?"
I nodded. "Well, that's one measurable

"form of the psychic vibrations we give
off. The vibrations attract certain souls
to our own during life and also at

"death. The energy we've generated
during life determines which level of
multiverse energy we attract at

"death. We've actually been travelling
through different multiverses where souls
with similar vibrations are guided."

Spying another construction area
with plywood barriers and a sign that
read, 'Under Construction', I asked Dante

what it was. His reply, "Oh, that's for new
sins which the inquisitive, creative
and resourceful human species is sure

"to invent someday. Man just hasn't thought
of them yet. I'm betting the new sins will
have something to do with artificial

"intelligence, or robotics, or else
biotechnology." "Oh, really," I
said, rolling my eyes. Dante just smirked at

me. Good thing he had a sense of humor.
"By the way," I said, "you wrote an entire
canto on the Suicides. You know, the

"one where the Suicides were turned into
trees, and every time one of their limbs would
break off, they'd bleed and cry out because God

"was punishing them for treating their own
bodies no better than they would treat a
plant." "I did not write that!" Dante snapped.

I liked him better the moment before.
"My censors compromised my work again!"
I braced myself for another rant. "The

"Church resented suicide because it
removed another dues-paying member
from its ranks. I mean, suicide is bad

"in itself. It's a violation of
the natural law of survival and
it traumatizes family and friends.

"But why would a kind and loving God damn
for all eternity a person who
was already living in his own Hell?"

But before I could answer he went on.
"You have to understand that the peasants
in my day were already living as

"if they were in some parts of Hell described
by the revisionist *Comedy*. Their
lives were hard, hungry, tragic and short-lived.

"The only ways the Church could convince them
to tithe was to promise them a better
afterlife, or else tell them their present

"suffering would last for eternity.
I mean, when you think about it, how can
a person be punished eternally?

"Ask someone with chronic pain and they'll
tell you that after a few years they could
adapt. Even some torture victims find

"ways to survive. Not only is a Hell
which is a punitive deterrent to
sin inconsistent with the idea of

"a loving Creator, but it's not too
efficient. Using up large portions of
universes for eternal prisons

"to punish sins that take place over the
few decades of a normal human life
is as wasteful as creating new souls

"by the millions. Nature recycles
water by way of evaporation
and rainfall. Why wouldn't the Creator

"conserve the energy that's present in
a reincarnating soul?" I had no
answer, I just waited patiently for

him to finish, then asked, "What is this place
we're approaching now?" He looked around as
if coming out of a trance and said, "Um

"yeah. This is the middle level of Hell.
It's like a minimum security
prison for sinners who aren't all that bad,

"they just refuse to leave their favorite
character defects behind when they die.
Because this is minimum security

"around here there are a few escapees
who make a nuisance of themselves when they
get lost and end up as poltergeists, ghosts,

"spirit possessions and such. Sometimes a
good exorcism brings 'em back and at
other times they either dread returning

"or they think they found an easier path,
or else by possessing a living soul
they can relive their beloved vices.

"Sex is usually at the top of
the list, but sometimes just being able
to smell flowers again is all they want.

"They're either too lazy or too fearful
to experience these sensations the
hard way -- by reincarnating again.

"And, of course, some shades here are always tuned
in to people who open the channels
through mediumship, séances, Ouija

"boards and other fortune telling methods.
Marilyn Monroe and Elvis are two
of peoples' preferred spirits to summon.

"I do wish they'd let those unfortunate
shades rest. It's so rude to summon spirits
back from the dead! It's like calling someone

"during an important meeting to sell
them a subscription or something. Then there
are those living souls who naturally

"vibrate on a spiritual level.
For them the reverse is true -- the spirits
can summon those living souls at will. Now

"those people who are able to attract
spirits from higher realms, at least, have some
protection." We came to a gate with a
battered sign, '..don all hope y ho enter..'.

Canto XIV

the incinerator, the suicides

"Oh, yeah," Dante countered to my unasked
question. "That sign had so much popular
appeal that they kept it even after

"most of the letters had worn off." The sign
also had some graffiti written on
it declaring that 'Socrates was here'.

"That Greek clique likes to tag everything," said
Dante. In the distance I could see two
towers with glowing red flames on the tops.

"What are those?" I asked, pointing. Dante glanced
in that direction and responded, "The
City of Dis was moved over there where

"they use it as an incinerator."
"The City of Dis?" I asked again. "Yeah.
In the old *Divine Comedy* it was

"the entrance to Hell proper. Renovators
looked over the crumbling infrastructure
and decided to salvage it for parts.

"They thought those two towers would make a nice
nostalgic entranceway to Hell's furnace."
I was almost afraid to ask what was

burning there. Dante answered anyway.
"Remember in the ring of the violent
criminals I said that some psychopaths

are so damaged they have to be destroyed?"
I nodded. "That's the way we destroy them
over there." I also saw a dump truck

drive towards the towers. "So some souls just
get burned up?" This time Dante nodded. "What
happens to them after they go through there?"

My Guide said, "They just get burned up. Gone. Not
even ashes are left behind. They can't
be allowed to reincarnate, they can't

"meet the standards for Purgatory, and
keeping them in Hell is not efficient.
It takes a lot of resources to train

"and maintain three shifts of personnel who
keep up with the torments. These mutated
souls can't even learn in Hell, just as they

"couldn't learn basic moral codes on Earth."
My mind raced back to freshman Chemistry.
"Thermodynamically speaking, it seems

"like their spiritual energy can't
just be destroyed like that. They must end up
somewhere," I argued. My Master replied,

"Hatred and ignorance actually
dissipate a lot of energy from
a soul. That energy becomes free to

"bind elsewhere, like to a Satan figure."
"That's scary," I vacillated. "It should
be," was his response. "That's why it's better

"to incinerate them and convert that
negativity into Hell's murky
atmosphere that you've seen so much of. Now

"a couple of serial killers, for
instance, were so leathery they needed
extra gasoline on the fire just to

"keep it from going out." He continued
to talk about some ethereal thing
or other. Meanwhile I found the only

comfortable spot I had seen since we
began our voyage. I sat, drinking in
the gloomy, stale air and stretching my legs.

"Why are you sitting?" He was impatient.
"My feet hurt," I whined. He practically yelled,
"Get up! We have a long way to go yet!"

I whined some more, then he said, "Do you want
to stay here?" I answered, "No-o-o-o, not really."
"Do I have to levitate you?! Let's go!"

Like a child running to catch up with its
mother I hurried to my feet saying,
"I'm sorry, I just…" He ignored me and

continued along the way saying, "This
is the region of the suicides."
Coming up was a not too unpleasant

field where scores of people sat with their eyes
closed. Some of them had wrapped makeshift blindfolds
over their eyes. They sat closely but there

was no conversation. In fact, the place
was unusually still. We came up
to one spirit whom Dante attempted

to engage in conversation. The shade
seemed to cringe at his questioning. "Why don't
you open your eyes?" Dante asked. "I don't

"want to see anything," came the response.
Dante's voice was gentle. "But you will be
able to find your way out of here if

"you just open your eyes and look." The shade
replied, "It's no use. There's no place to go."
"But if you go on to Purgatory,"

Dante argued, "you can work through those things
that brought you here." "I'm OK where I am,"
came the stubborn answer. To another

spirit my Guide said, "Why don't you open
your eyes and see what's available to
you?" The retort: "There isn't anything

"for me." And from another the response
was, "In Purgatory I'll just have to
go through it all over again." Dante

gently said, "All of your trials were just
tests that you needed to pass and you were
winning until you suddenly gave up."

"I'm too ashamed," was another reply.
"The pain will come back," was yet another.
"I'll have to face those people," another

spirit revealed and so it went from soul to
soul to soul. We walked onward and he asked
several spirits why they didn't at

least talk to each other about problems
and give each other support. The answers
were all variations of, 'too painful.'

Then Dante tried asking some souls, "What did
you need to keep from killing yourself" The
replies ranged from 'I don't know' to 'Leave

'me alone'. Dante said, "When they can give
an answer to that question, then they are
ready to open their eyes and move on."

We resumed our trip to see 'Self Pity'.

Canto XV

the self-pitying

I felt great relief as we left that realm
of souls who couldn't see the miracle
of life itself. The next realm didn't prove

to be much livelier. It was filled with
wandering souls who beat their breasts and wailed
about their misfortunes. Several got

into misfortune-wailing contests where
the loser gained even more to begrudge.
A few had been given tools to build

a better environment for themselves
but they used the tools instead to build a
pulpit from which they could complain better.

Another competition between two
pulpits arose and we paused to listen.
"If it hadn't been for those foreigners

"stealing my job I could have amounted
to something instead of going to jail."
Not to be outdone a second speaker

interjected, "I even formed a hate
group and voted for hate candidates but
that liberal conspiracy out East

"spread their lies and propaganda and my
party was defeated." "Sounds like Florence,"
said Dante. A third soul took his pulpit:

"Oh wicked Time! Oh thief of all that lives!
When we are given youth we own it all.
The old ones just exist, and always have.

"We never see that blind conveyor belt
that moves us relentlessly through our Age
until the old ones die and we are left.

"We never think that we will be replaced
by young ones just as ignorant as we,
who own the world now, just as we once did.

"A flower proudly blooms amid decay.
It grew from seed and now produces seeds,
then watches its own bottom leaves turn brown...

"No, Hell is not a wicked place where all
incorrigible people go to rot.
It's a believable infinity

"A dread more real than promises of bliss
which always lie beyond our grasping reach.
Our bodies die, and then our memories.

"But Hell, at least, allows our sin to live."
"Oh, dear," I exclaimed. The spirit just shrugged.
"Oh dear — what," asked Dante, "the verse or the

"sentiment?" Turning to the dead poet
My Guide and Teacher simply said, "Needs work."
Turning to me he whispered, "This realm reeks

"of unpublished writers." The first speaker
complained, "Just what does all that gibberish
have to do with *my* problems?" "You think *you*

"had problems..." a second speaker yelled
and was interrupted by a chorus
of angry orators who presented

their woes more loudly than the rest. "Excuse
me, Dante," I said, trying to be heard,
"granted, these people are obnoxious but

"how did they warrant a sentence in Hell?"
He answered, "A bad attitude alone
usually just earns one a place in

"Purgatory. These spirits, however
caused harm to others because of their bad
attitudes. For example, that soul there,"

he pointed, "harassed women 'til they lost
promotions and even some jobs because
he was convinced they had an advantage

"over him. And that one," pointing to the
first speaker, "spread her self-indulgent slop
over her kids and marred their adulthood.

"If her life was so bad she should have used
birth control rather than force another
soul to endure her misery. Jesus

"even warns, in *Matthew*, about causing
a little one to sin. Then, of course, you
heard Mister Hate Group give his spiel. He urged

"that group to violence and he barely
escaped that realm we visited before
because the group kept all their threats verbal."

Dante continued, "Sin is not black or
white – there is a spectrum. For the most part
people who keep their impulses and fears

"under control can escape sin, even
though the impulse can be overwhelming.
But then those people need to follow up

"and examine those harmful ponderings
that afflict them and try to prevent them
from recurring." I said to him, "I thought

"Satan causes evil thoughts." He replied,
"Satan is caused by evil thoughts, as I
said before. It's hard for you to grasp

"that, isn't it?" I nodded. Resuming:
"No, the conflict comes from our intellect
which is more powerful than we believe

"and which needs to be trained from childhood on.
Formal religions can be vital to
guide young people in their morality

"until their consciousness matures enough
to take over the controls." A fist fight
broke out among the orators and they

started flinging their podiums at each
other, which brought on a roaring legion
of winged motorcyclists to break it up.

"If you've had enough fun here, let's move on."

Canto XVI

the hotheads

We ventured up a cliff to a plateau
where, oddly, Hell was heating up again.
Perspiring heavily, I enquired of

Dante why that was. "It's all the hotheads
here," my Teacher explained. "Every time
they open their mouths, venomous flames join

"their words as they screech their opinions to
the world, not caring what the opposing
side may have to say." A shade, however

whom Dante said would soon be leaving, said
to me, "Listen to these useless rants. One
is Democrat, one Republican, one

"is Labor Party, another is from
the Socialists and most don't care enough
to vote – they just want to scream. None of them

"seem to realize that while they heat the
air with their bad breath, the world is warming
past the danger point, it doesn't matter

"who is sleeping with whom (as long as they
leave the kids alone) and no matter how
many bombs we drop we cannot make ourselves

"safe from terrorists who want *their* homelands
to be sovereign, too. In life I wasted
so much time and breath trying to convince

"others that my views are the right ones that
I didn't notice my friends and family
falling away. I didn't watch my kids

"grow up. I didn't stop to enjoy those
lovely nights in Spring, and I didn't see
my wife grow old. I couldn't watch the news

"without yelling at a lifeless TV
screen and I didn't realize how scared
my children were of the world I described

"to them. I sit here now in this lonely
place trying to remember everything
I missed because of my politicking.

"I wish I could apologize to my
kids when they were teens, wrap them in my arms
and tell them that the future I had thrust

"upon them would be OK. It will work
out all right just as it always has. My
daughter now is in the region of the

"suicides and my son is heading for
the violent criminal section. If
I could only visit him in a dream

"or haunt him as Hamlet's father did, I
could tell him how wrong I was and how much
I've always loved him. And I would pray for

"my little Anna to get her out of
her own trap." The spirit wept bitterly
as my Beloved Guide touched his shoulder.

"He's ready!" Dante shouted to no one
in particular. And in a flash the
weeping shade was gone. A broad grin filled my

Master's face as he turned to me and said,
"It won't be easy for him, but his spot
in Purgatory has been waiting for

"quite awhile now. I always feel such an
overwhelming sensation of love and
peace when I see a spirit graduate."

Our peaceful moment didn't last too long
because, once the initial shock of the
disappearance was gone, the other shades

fell back into ranting and raving. The
air heated up again. One spirit yelled,
"Those g___d___ liberals have even ruined

"Hell. It's all a play to break the spirit
of patriots like me!" And another
"You're no patriot — you're a Fascist pig!"

Soon the assembled multitude parted
itself into the Commie Pinko Fags
versus the Reactionary Mother

F----rs, and then just as quickly transformed
themselves into the Radical Left and
the Extremist Right, then Pro-Life versus

Pro-Choice, then Conservationists versus
Pro-Industry Activists, then they all
jumped into opposing camps on climate

change, evolution, Ford versus Chevy,
Isolationism versus Regime
Change, Christian versus Muslim and then the

Christians partitioned into Catholic
against Protestant while the Muslims split
into Sunni, Shi'a, Sufi and a

few others. Just as the arguing was
heating up to a comfortable boil
the Hell's motorcycle club zoomed in to

quiet everybody down because the
crowd had become engorged on their own
adrenaline and the fight had become

too much fun. With the cracking of whips, the
awful thudding of chains slamming into
dead souls and subsequent screams of torment,

each contestant retreated into its
own little foxhole. For a short time. Then
one lone voice cried out, "It's all your fault you

"faggot-loving, baby-killing liars!"
The retreating bikers wheeled back around
to whip everyone who was jumping out

of their foxhole to sermonize again.
A pager went off and the angelic
motorcyclists had to run off to quell

another dispute in a different
part of Hell. Dante grabbed me and shouted,
"The bikers are getting more staffing soon.

"Let's get out of here before it heats up!"

Canto XVII

the lustful

A helicopter appeared from nowhere
to lift us out of the riot below
just in time to avoid flying objects.

With a sigh, Dante said, "This new transport
system is so nice. Virgil always had
to waste so much time coaxing Geryon

"into carrying tourists on its back
without eating them." Soon the air cooled down
to a temperature that was almost

tolerable and we landed on a
narrow ridge which overlooked a valley.
A fanning breeze moved the hot air without

any real cooling, which made this region,
too, quite uncomfortable. "It's Hell, you
know," Dante remarked, reading my sad thoughts.

After awhile I realized that the breeze
was being created by a swirling
mass of souls who were being blown around

beneath the precipice on which we stood.
The two of us observed them for awhile.
Then Master Dante said, "When I went through

"this trip with Virgil, the Wanton Lustful
were on the second ring of Hell below
the Virtuous Heathen. These passionate

"souls, however, probably never cared
and maybe even never knew that they
had been transferred for the Remodeling."

In contrast to the moaning I had heard
thus far, the vocalization I was
hearing from this crowd had a unique tone.

It was worse than living across a wall
from a honeymooning couple. Dante
seemed nonplussed as he explained, "This is the

"new ring of the Wanton. Here dead souls are
being called to task for their unrestrained
sexuality in life. Even my

"censors must have blushed while they figured out
how to sugar-coat this stuff and clean it
up." For the first time I heard him belly

laugh. "Sorry", he said. "I still get a kick
out of envisioning some celibate
monk struggle to read and censor my work."

A flurry of naked bodies soared past
us with sighs and exclamations of pure
orgasmic passion. I looked at Dante.

"This doesn't seem very Hellish," I said,
"except for those of us who have to watch."
I hoped the Poet couldn't see my blush.

"Actually," Dante countered, "their sin
lies in being unable to find their
real passion. Anyone who is stuck in

"a rut like sex addiction or drugs or
gambling or anything else that merely
tickles the dopamine receptors fails

"to savor the ecstatic reward that
comes from purpose, growth and enlightenment.
Now, those who harm others in their pursuit

"of a dopamine high end up in a
different region. Instant Karma is
seldom a victimless crime." I pondered,

"It looks like it would be difficult to
persuade someone to leave this area."
Dante shook his head, "You would be surprised.

"Multiple orgasms actually
become quite unpleasant after a few
hundred years." Suddenly in front of us

a soul spun off from the group like someone
who was playing 'crack the whip' on ice skates
and it just as suddenly disappeared.

"Purgatory," Dante shrugged. "See? It's not
all fun and games." "I guess not," I said as
another soul flew past and vanished. "May

"I ask a question?" My Leader replied,
"Of course!" I hesitated because I
knew how sensitive he was about the

Divine Comedy. "In your manuscript,"
I began. I could see him tense up and
take a deep breath, releasing it slowly.

"Yes, go ahead. It's OK." Well there was
a lot written about the horrible
burning punishments some of your friends had

"to endure ostensibly because of
sodomy…" A tear filled Dante's eye as
he whispered, "Brunetto Latini, my

"dear teacher. The manuscript re-writers
portrayed that gentle soul with burned off skin,
trudging eternally in a fiery

"sandpit. How can men of God even think
of such torture for someone just because,
unlike themselves, he was caught in the act?"

This time it was my sympathetic hand
which reached out for Dante's shoulder. He turned
away briefly to hide more tears, then he

calmed himself. "Love is love and lust is lust.
To abuse one's body for lust is sin.
To use the body for love is to bless

"the Creator because it can lead to
procreation. Homosexuals, for
the most part, were the opposite gender

"during their past incarnation and this
time around they haven't had enough time
to adjust to the gender conversion.

"Brunetto, my friend, may you forgive them."

Canto XVIII

miscellaneous sins, the co-dependent

We walked away from that unpleasant scene.
Politely I pretended not to see
that extra bulge in Dante's loosely draped

garment. Clearing his throat my Leader said,
"The Church has many clergy in that group.
Their ban on normal marital sex had

"created centuries of aberrant
sexual release. Young acolytes, of
course, were victimized quite frequently. But

"not too many people realize how
sexually sadistic many witch
interrogations were. The *Malleus*

"*Maleficarum* details which parts of
the body had to be examined with
meticulous care in order to find

"those markings which betrayed the young woman
to be a consort of Satan. She'd have
to be tied and stripped naked, of course, in

"order to detect those moles and scars and
birthmarks. Then they'd save her soul by burning
her - and any accusations of rape."

Silently we trudged along a gloomy
path toward our next destination. I
broke the silence by asking, "Your epic

"poem mentions sins like 'barratry', 'sloth',
'augury', 'simony', 'alchemy' and
sinners like 'peculators', 'usurers'

"and 'heresiarchs'. " He nodded. "And your
question is...?" "Well, forgive me for being
so stupid, but what are 'barrators' and

"'peculators' and such?" He cleared his throat
again and confessed, "I have no idea,
but whatever they are, don't do 'em. They're

"sinful." He seemed relieved at nearing our
next step in that harrowing pilgrimage,
and he quickly changed the subject. The

next parallel universe we entered was
a strange little valley with souls swinging
to and fro, seemingly in pairs. Their cords

did not seem to be tied tightly, but yet
the couples behaved as if they had no
choice but to bump into each other like

gravity balls suspended from that toy
apparatus one sees on so many
executives' desks. First one soul would swing

toward the other who waited, inert,
then it would slam into the other, curse,
and harangue while the other swung away.

Immediately they repeated the
process, slammed together, cursed, repeated
and exchanged insults during their brief time

together. I told Dante, "You've shown me
some gory areas, some scary ones
and some areas that were disgusting.

"But this realm is just downright weird." Dante
responded, "No weirder than the lives they
chose to live on Earth. This is the realm of

"the Co-Dependent. In life they torment
each other, scare their kids with their fights,
then go back for more passionate drama.

"Perhaps the weirdest part is that these souls
are so addicted to each other that
they patiently wait here after death for

"the other partner to rejoin them. And
if the living partner finds another,
as they frequently do in bars, then all

"the souls knock each other about as you
see here. It would be rather humorous
if it wasn't so sad and frustrating."

Sure enough, there were groups of four, five and
more from serial marriages on Earth
crashing into one another, yelling

curses and insults, then pulling away.
Like a perpetual motion machine
powered by mutual hate and passion

they attacked each other, sometimes as a
group, but were unable to stay away
from each other. From the swaying spirits

we could hear things like, "You're the reason why
I drink," and "You're worse than a little kid,"
"You need to change," and, "You're the one who's wrong."

Time and again the same sentiments were
repeated with similar words and no
resolution to the arguments. Then

I watched a bickering couple pause to
search for an ex, then return to the fight.
"They're starting to drive me nuts," I muttered.

"Oh, this is nothing," said Dante. "On Earth
couples stop long enough to have more kids."
Shocked, I asked him, "What happens to those kids?

"What did the children do to deserve a
life with these souls?" His answer, "The spirits
from Purgatory who volunteer to

"incarnate with difficult parents can
often serve as spiritual teachers.
It is part of their own development.

"These are the youngsters you see who grow up
in alcoholic homes, or abusive
or broken homes or trauma and become

"responsible adults. They are old souls
who have reincarnated many times
and are working off Karma through service."

I said, "This keeps getting more confusing."

Canto XIX

escapism

We strolled into an area which was
inhabited by warehouses full of
computer screens with shades staring into

them and wiggling gaming devices. Not
only did the spirits accept being
there, but they were so focused on their screens

that they seemed oblivious to us and
to everything else around them. "They don't
seem to realize that they are in Hell,"

I told Dante. He said, "They will in a
minute." Then stooping down to pick up a
power cord, he glanced at me and unplugged

the gaming stations. Immediately
dozens, maybe hundreds of souls stood up
amid loud complaints and groans. My Teacher

explained, "This is the escapist region.
In order to avoid relationships
and commitments to other people these

"souls chose to bury themselves in their games.
The only socializing they do is
online. So, at random intervals for

"undetermined periods of time the
power is cut and then restored. These souls
need to reengage with others and this

"torment is there to remind them of that.
Previous generations who buried
themselves in reading and solitary

"pursuits to the exclusion of people
who loved them and needed their attention
are represented elsewhere. It's

"not easy to maintain relationships
with people around us — to fulfill their
needs and make our own needs known to them. As

"I explained to you earlier, sometimes
sin is just taking the easy way out.
Further along we'll see those people who

"have given up on life in other ways
that are just short of suicide. They are
the Apathetic and the Chronically

"Miserable. Rather than take any
risks, or reach out for help, they choose to dwell
in their own ruts. There, you can see some of

"them off to the right." Dante pointed to
a hill littered with souls lounging around,
not speaking, not moving and not even

interacting with celestial helpers
who prodded them occasionally and
yelled in their ears. I turned to my Mentor

and said, "This *does* look like the Suicides'
realm." The Master answered back, "Part of the
soul's growth is to learn how to function with

"other souls. You'll see when you travel to
Purgatory and Paradise just how
important it is to learn nurturing

"communication, assertiveness and
respect for others' needs. These are the same
souls who feel an emptiness, loneliness

"and who seek relief in drugs, alcohol
and sometimes in thrill-seeking behavior.
Now this next area," he pointed to

the gateway as we approached it, "is where
our escapists don't even have enough
ambition to sit behind a book or

"a computer screen." Entering through that
open filigree wrought iron portal
which was latched but unlocked and easily

escaped, we stepped around those spirits we
had seen from afar. They did, indeed, look
quite apathetic. Dante spoke, "This sin

"used to be referred to as sloth. It is,
in fact, the basis of many other
sins. The passions can lead to homicide

"and rape, but sloth can make people lessen
life's workload by double-crossing others,
stealing, lying and even becoming

"addicted to substances or habits
that substitute for genuine living.
Obviously the people around this

"moocher are harmed, but the freeloader, too
cheats himself out of the rewarding things
in life." A divine motorcyclist got

one of the apathetic souls to move
out of the way when he roared past, but the
spirit slumped back into its previous

manner as soon as the biker left. "Now
another variation of this sin,"
Dante said, continuing his guided

tour, "is off to our left. These spirits are
the Chronically Miserable — not to
be confused with depression. Depressed souls

"are a different category. No, the
miserable ones are souls who delight
in ruining other people's days. Let me

"show you." Going up to a scowling soul
the Teacher said, "Good afternoon." "What's so
damn good about it?" the spirit bellowed.

Turning to me, Dante asked, "Would you like
to see more?" "No, I think I get the idea,"
I answered. "But who are these flagellants?"

A line of hooded, robed figures, who were
whipping themselves as they walked, crossed our path.
His reply, "These souls managed to avoid

"success by sabotaging whatever
they attempted and then blaming it all
on bad luck or on their acquaintances."

I asked, "But why run from success?" Replied
Dante, "With success comes obligations.
A successful businessman needs to take

"care of employees and consistently
provide whatever goods or services
he has promised. A successful parent

"must also put a lot of work into
raising their child while sacrificing their
own needs. Sometimes success can be scary.

"Let's move on now to see what Greed looks like."

Canto XX

the greedy and the gluttonous

"Let's see now," Dante mumbled to himself,
"have we missed anyone?" He retrieved the
maps from inside his robe. "Sloth-check. Hubris-check

"Lust-yes. Wrath and Envy-OK. Greed and
Gluttony-coming up." Then turning back
toward me my Guide said, "The greedy and

"the gluttonous like to hang together
to see if one group is hoarding something
that the other group wants. We will have to

"levitate over some areas to
keep from getting buried in all the trash."
"Levitate?!" I exclaimed, "how cool is that?"

Dante just ignored me and kept walking.
Soon we reached the door of a neon-lit
casino. "Hang on," he ordered me. Then

cautiously Dante opened the latch. Like
Fibber McGee's closet a huge pile of
coins spilled out, leaving us a small entrance

at the top of the pile. Typical sounds
of a casino rang out-musical
jingling and coins dropping. Looking around

I saw that the floor of the casino
was covered five or six feet high with coins.
On top of the coins sat gamblers who were

fixated on the one-armed bandits that
they and the staff had to lift above the
coin piles in order to keep playing.

The speculators seemed oblivious
to their environment except for slot
machines which were set to win every time.

"Pardon me, Dante," I began slowly,
"but this is another area that
doesn't seem very Hellish. I mean slots

"that are set to always win?" He nodded,
then pointed at one of the gamblers. "Do
you see what that spirit is eating?" I glanced

in that direction. Sure enough the soul
was grabbing coins from the pile he sat on
and stuffed them into his mouth. Dante said,

"He cannot tear himself away from the
prospect of more winnings long enough to
eat, yet he is desperately hungry

"for real food. Look more closely underneath
him." I did as directed and almost
choked. My Master then added, "Well, you know

"what goes in must come out." He turned to the
spirit and asked, "Why are you staying here?"
The shade replied, "I'm in Heaven! Look at

"this winning streak!" Dante argued back, "It
doesn't look like you're winning anything.
How many tokens are you sitting on?"

"I have no idea," the shade answered, "but
I want more." From the next room a portly
spirit and an emaciated one

peeked over to see what all the gamblers
were sitting on. My Teacher explained, "Those
are the Gluttons I told you about." I

directed my gaze at the two spirits
in the doorway and said, "I understand
why one soul would be obese, but why would

"the other soul be so skinny?" Dante
replied, "Gluttony is actually the
abuse of food. One eats excessively

"and wastes what's left even though he should have
shared his bounty with those who are starving.
The other starves herself in the midst of

"plenty because she thinks it makes her more
attractive. Both of them have sinned because
they did not utilize treatment programs

"designed for their special problems, or else
they left their programs without following
the guidelines they were taught. These other souls,"

he pointed to some other spirits who
congregated at the entrance, "have glutted
themselves on drugs, and the ones next to them,"

he pointed again, "were addicted to
exercise. It's amazing, actually,
how many addictions humans can harm

"themselves with — eating toilet paper or
cleaning products, having unwarranted
plastic surgeries, buying and hoarding

"items they cannot possibly use or
even find storage for. All of this is
to run away from their hang-ups rather

"than face the hole they have dug for themselves,
and then do the hard work they need to do
in order to stay out of that hole." I

asked him, "But why were these spirits given
the desire to climb into that rut
in the first place? It's like some sort of curse

"was put on them while on Earth and that's not
fair." The Teacher answered, "Remember what
we discussed about tests and our need to

"pass those tests in order to move on. These
souls were unfortunate enough to die
while still in the grip of their addictions.

"They do have the option of repenting
and then retaking their tests, with coaching,
in Purgatory, but they are too scared

"to accept the offer. Many of the
spirits you see here struggled with the same
habituations in previous lives

"and didn't pass their exams then, either.
Now a different approach has to be
attempted to break them out of their bad

"habits by giving them a stint here in
Hell." "It seems rather harsh," I said. "There were
harsh consequences for their families,"

he replied, uncharacteristically
cold and judgmental. "Sins like murder and
swindling are easy to condemn, but these

"more subtle evils often elicit
the kind of pity from others that is
equally destructive. Any questions?"

I just shook my head and asked what was next.

Canto XXI

the ladder back to Earth

Dante was in a noticeably dour
mood as we walked along another path.
So I asked him, "Is it something I said?"

As if startled awake from a daydream
he replied, "Huh? Um, no. Not this time. It's
just that we're approaching the uppermost

"regions now — 'The Hell of Reality'.
This is probably the roughest part to
witness because it is the Hell you see

"on the evening news every day." I shrugged,
"The news is usually bad, but I am
normally able to survive it."

His reply, "That's because you are safely
sitting at home with a television
screen protecting you. There's that luxury

"of denial you won't get here." Coming
up ahead was an incredibly long
ladder that stretched upwards to a patch of

blue sky. I found myself running toward
it like a little kid. Dante didn't
even try to call me back. He knew I

would lose my enthusiasm once I
reached the foot of that ladder and looked up.
Dante was a very wise Conductor.

And so we climbed. And climbed. And climbed some more.
"Hey Dante?" I asked. "Do you remember
that tar pit in the region of those who

"are violent to the Earth?" "Forget it,"
he snapped. "I'm not carrying you this time!"
"Sorry I asked." My legs felt rubbery.

"Couldn't they have made an elevator
that also goes up?" "Shut up and climb," his
patience was obviously growing thin.

Finally we reached the top. "You can give
me my cloak now," was all he said. I had
almost forgotten I still had it on.

"Thanks for loaning it to me," I offered,
hoping to cheer him up a bit. "That pit
we just came from had more radiation

"than Chernobyl. Your skin would have fallen
off in shreds without the cloak." I didn't
comment. I just appreciated the

first pleasant set of smells I'd known since I
started that strange trip. Expecting the worst,
which was all Dante had shown me thus far,

I studied my environment, looking
for all the inevitable horrors.
Instead I saw blue skies, fluffy clouds, green

shimmering trees filled with singing birds and
a lovely suburban scene with people
walking on sidewalks and cars on the street.

I looked cautiously over at Dante.
"So far everything looks normal," I said.
Suddenly the earth shifted and gave way

beneath our feet. Dante grabbed me, shouting,
"Sinkhole!" I screamed, "No! Not Hell again!" We
fell at least twenty feet before landing

in the mud along with crumbled asphalt
and a Volkswagen bus. It took a few
moments for the earth to settle again.

It took a few more moments for my nerves
to settle again. It didn't take too
long, however, for a crowd to peer at

us from the rim of the sinkhole. "Hello!"
I hollered from the bottom. "They can't hear
us," said Dante. So I yelled louder, "Get

"us out of here!" and I waved my arms with
crazy sweeping gestures. "They can't see us,
either," Dante said calmly. Then I heard

someone at the top of the hole mention
the minivan that was there with us
and someone else reassured the others

that there was nobody inside. "Hello!"
I yelled again. Finally Dante said,
"Save your breath. We're invisible to them."

"Well why the heck are we invisible?!
We're in a sinkhole and we need to get
out!" (I had forgotten for a moment

who I was talking to.) My Mentor seemed
to understand my panic. The spectators
at the rim of the hole assembled, then

dissipated at their leisure when they
had finally seen enough. I felt like
a sideshow attraction, but Dante just

calmly studied his maps. "OK," he said
at last. "This region starts out with a three-
sixty panoramic presentation

"which uses the sides of the sinkhole as
a projection screen. The good news is that
the soundtrack is supposed to be pretty

"good." I muttered to myself, "I don't like
movies and I don't like music. I want
to go home and have a beer." "Sorry," he

said, "the concession stand doesn't sell beer."
"Of course it doesn't," I grumbled as the
music started. "This is Hell after all."

"Oh, really," said Dante, rolling his eyes.

Canto XXII

Impermanence of Earth

The walls of the sinkhole lit up as with
a movie screen, flickering at first, then
joined with a rather poor sound track that whined

to its full sound. Too many violins.
The narrator of the video then
began, "You are in the uppermost crust

"of the Earth. The Biosphere, which is where
all life is found, is only eighty miles
thick. Would you like to open a viewing

"area beneath your feet so you can
see how incredibly thin this layer
of Earth is relative to its core?" "NO!"

I screamed and lunged at Dante to throw my
arms and legs around him. "All right then," the
narrator continued, "you'll have to take

"my word for it. However, do look at
the top four or five inches of dirt at
the top of the sinkhole." I obeyed while

Dante peeled me off and set me back on
the ground. "These top few inches of Earth's thin
crust are where all food is produced. Notice

"how pale and sandy the dirt is under
the asphalt." I nodded. "In the last five
decades almost one-third of arable

"land has been exhausted and turned into
desert, with vital topsoil being blown
into the oceans. Yet during this time

"the total population has more than
doubled." I was surrounded with pictures
of parched deserts, starving babies, crowded

cities and sprawling hectares of oil fields.
"The Green Revolution provided a
temporary fix to the problem of

"feeding a burgeoning population,
but with a projected population
nearing 10 billion people by the

"end of this century, it is doubtful
that a similar breakthrough can occur
again." Now the video display showed

oceanscapes with dead coral reefs and a
montage of beaches covered with dead fish.
"A few decades ago scientists hoped

"to mine the seas for new sources of food.
But with rising atmospheric temps and
acidification of the oceans

"from dissolved CO2 created by
industrial output, several fish
species' numbers are dwindling." The movie

returned to scenes of disappearing seas
and dried up riverbeds. "The sinkhole you
are standing in was once an aquafer."

Then the video flickered to an end.
"I've already seen this film on public
television," I complained. "Will you please

"stop whining?" he scolded. "Jeez, you're getting
on my nerves!" "Whatever," I sighed. Then, "So
what's next?" Scanning his maps, my Leader said,

"This upper region of Hell is laid out
like the spokes of a wheel, and we are at
the center of it. There are portals leading

"out from the hub, where we are standing now,
which we need to explore." Climbing on top
of the Volkswagen I asked, "Can't we just

"crawl out of the sinkhole and catch a ride
back home? I'll grill you a burger and find
some nice, cold beer. Do you like Bud?" He sniffed

at me and said, "I'm dead, remember? Dead
people don't eat. Now focus. You are near
the first portal right now. The minivan

"is the twelve o'clock landmark. From there we
go to the three o'clock position and
feel for an opening in the side of

"this cave-in." He stuffed the map back into
his robes and felt along the wall. All of
a sudden a small demon burst through the

portal and somehow snatched Dante's map from
his robe, then disappeared back into the
wall from where he came. Dante and I both

dove into a sand-plus-asphalt wall which
surprisingly gave way, like an Alice
in Wonderland gimmick. The demon could

be seen running ahead of us in a
misty corridor which didn't seem to
lead anywhere. I battled to keep up

with Dante, who in turn seemed to have the
demon in his sights yet. Then the mist cleared.
Neither the demon nor the stolen map

could be seen, but we did find ourselves
in what appeared to be a theater,
with a family feature on the marquee.

"It looks like we made it to our first stop."

Canto XXIII

active shooter in a theater

Grateful to be out of the sinkhole
I looked around at my new surroundings.
Dante and I were sitting in a dark

theater with tubs of popcorn, a drink,
and children's voices being hushed by their
moms. A few voices still chattered and were

hushed again as the movie screen lit up
and the soundtrack began. "Another flick
about global devastation?" I asked

my Mentor. "Ssshh!" he hissed, and dipped into
his popcorn. "I thought that dead people don't
eat," I hissed back. Whatever remark he

made was drowned out by the opening
actions. It was a cowboy movie and
some bad guy was shooting at the townsfolk.

There were a few more gunshots coming from
the screen and then suddenly Dante pulled me
down to the floor, whispering, "Get down and

"be quiet!" "What the…?" I started to say
until I realized that the shots were
being fired inside the theater.

The movie's soundtrack was accompanied
now by a couple of screams from the crowd.
Most of the audience was still quiet,

apparently believing that all the
gunshots were coming from the movie screen.
Suddenly it was as if everyone

woke up at the same time and their screams filled
the theater, supplemented by the
'pop-pop' of live rounds. Dante shoved my head

lower beneath the seats where I had to
endure sticky old cola and stale gum.
The sounds of people wrestling their way

out of the uncooperative folding
seats joined the screams and the gunshots. It was
still a flickering darkness inside as

the movie blared casually. "Mommy!"
'pop-pop-pop', "Help!" "Don't shoot her!" 'pop' "Mommy!"
A musical score from the screen was a

sinister backdrop for the drama in
the room. "Turn on the damned lights for chrissake!"
It took a while for the projector crew

to catch on to what was happening, so
the gunshots from the screen continued to
join the gunshots in the room. Finally

someone turned on the lights so I could raise
my head enough to look back toward the
aisle. All I could see was a pair of

trousered boots strolling past my row. A few shots
were much louder now because they were right
over my head. Dante had kept his hand

on my leg the whole time and squeezed it a
bit harder now, signaling me to stay
still. "Mommy!" 'pop-pop' and the child's voice was

hushed. Still the screams and the clunking of seats
and the cries for help rang out with more shots.
I wondered how many guys there were. I

wondered where the cops could be. I wondered
what I was doing there. Someone in the
row behind me thumped loudly against the

creaking seat and whimpered. 'pop-pop' Her cry
became a groan. 'pop-pop' Then she was still.
More stickiness plastered itself into

my hair. I didn't dare move in the dim
light, but I could see from the one eye - which
I had kept open - that the trousered boots

were moving away. I thought I'd heard the
sound of a reload, but I wasn't sure.
At last I heard the faint sound of sirens

in the distance. I hoped they were for us.
The siren sound, however, just set off
another wave of rapid gunfire. I

realized that with the theater lights
up, the shooter could see his prey better.
My legs were cramping up from lying still

pretending to be dead. The siren sounds
grew closer and were joined by more sirens.
The stickiness on the floor was warm and

uncomfortable. I thought I'd heard a
soft moan come from the row behind me, but
it was coming instead from another

row. The police must have been parked outside,
judging by the sirens. Why weren't they here
I wondered. Then, above the moans and the

soft groans coming from the room I heard doors
crash open. "Police! Drop your weapon!" I
started to get up but Dante hissed, "Stay

"down! You can still get killed in the crossfire!"
Sure enough there was now a full barrage
of gunshots whizzing overhead, then it

was all hushed. Soft moaning from several
locations split the silence. Finally
Dante let me get up and look around.

"Let's go this way," he said, pulling my
arm as I glanced behind us. "Oh my God,"
escaped from my parched mouth. Dante pulled me

past dozens of bloodied people who were
draped in various death postures around
overturned theater seats and the floor.

I fought Dante to look backward at them.

"What did we do to deserve this?" I asked.

"Nothing," Dante answered. "We're innocent."

We left and crawled into an ambulance.

Canto XXIV

the ambulance, ER

"We're not all going to fit in here," I
said as the ambulance screamed through traffic.
"Inhale," Dante ordered. As I did so

I could see that the medics were able
to do their work as if we weren't there. Then
they quickly took vital signs and started

an IV on an unconscious little
girl who was drenched in blood. "Can't they see us?"
I asked, not taking my eyes off the child.

Dante answered, "Can't see us, can't hear us,
just like before." Angry, I barked, "You mean
in the theater? Why didn't you tell

"me? I could have tackled that shooter and
stopped this rampage!" We arrived at the door
of the Emergency Room and ran with

the gurney into the trauma bay. We
were immediately joined by a team
of nurses, a few cops, some hospital

staff from other departments and a young
ER doctor who was struggling to stay
calm amid the chaos of multiple

gunshot victims. He called back to the desk
nurse, "Activate Mass Casualties!" She
busied herself on the phone while the girl's

family sorted her out from the rest
of the victims. A man who appeared to
be a chaplain led the hysterical

family aside. "Will she make it?" I
asked. Dante shook his head and continued
to survey the ER, as if looking

for something. "Twenty one injured," he said,
"and eleven killed, including five kids."
"Can we leave here?" I begged, my eyes misting.

"Not yet," Dante stated. "These people are
the lucky ones who have access to clean
water, medicines and doctors. Let me

"show you some other suffering patients.
He drew aside the curtain surrounding
an ER bed and, like some Ghost of

Christmas Present, a vision appeared to
me of a mother struggling to carry
her AIDS-stricken son along primitive

dirt roads to the nearest clinic. He cried
out in pain after each bump in the road
caught a wheel of her cart. She, too, wept as

she tugged at their cart, hoping against hope
that he would survive the trip. His diaper
was soiled but there was no clean water to

bathe him. Dante pointed in a different
direction toward a ghetto child who
held the hand of his dead drug addict mom.

Then he pointed to torture victims locked
in a cell where, one by one, several
died. Relentlessly he made me look at

refugees who were drowning because the
boat which was supposed to carry them to
freedom instead capsized. Then he showed me

the faces of two people who were trapped
under a pile of rubble following
and earthquake. Only their fingertips could

touch as they whispered encouragement to
each other day after day after day.
They were never found, he told me. Then he

showed me a mother who cried while taking
care of her severely handicapped son.
He showed me a woman who tried to get

rid of the voices in her head with a
knife, and a man whose arm was crushed while he
was at work trying to earn a living.

On and on, mercilessly, the visions
came – more natural disasters wiping
out entire towns, more victims of crime,

more crippling and disabling diseases,
more sorrow for lost loved ones, more children
stunted by hunger, sickness, bad water.

"Why are you doing this to me?" I sobbed.
"Watch and learn," he said sternly. "Listen and
learn. All of this has to be fixed someday."

"This is all so unfair!" I whimpered. "Why
is God letting it all be so unfair?"
Dante pushed the curtain back where it was

and we were once again in the ER.
He told me, "Because we haven't learned how
to fix everything yet." The little girl's

family were now gathered around her,
weeping inconsolably. Dante placed
his hand on my back and led me away.

We could hear the desk nurse complain to the
nursing supervisor that the second
floor was refusing any more admits.

"It's not fair!" she told her boss. "We're *all* swamped!"

Canto XXV

the second floor

I looked around at the scene before us.
Surprisingly, Dante also scanned the
area, unlike his typical self.

"Is something wrong?" I asked. "Yeah, we're in Hell,"
he snapped. "And what am I supposed to do
about that?!" I snapped back. He glared at me.

"You see any demons pass by?" he asked
finally. "About three feet tall, black, batwings,
snaky tail, ugly puss, carrying a

"map that I desperately need to get
us through here?" "Uh, oh." "Yeah, uh, oh," he said.
"So what do we do?" I asked. My legs were

getting rubbery again. He shrugged. "Pray
for guidance and then follow our instincts.
Remember that when you are lost — pray and

"listen for that inner voice. Discernment
is the key. You need to learn how to tune

out distractions so you can discern the
"true voice." I was actually too scared
to hear what he was saying. Instead I
stood frozen where we were. A nurse scurried

past us and Dante said, "Let's follow her."
She didn't appear to see us as she
gently knocked on a door, then entered the

room. Lying on a hospital bed was
a woman whose legs were permanently stuck
in a wheelchair position, and whose hands

were frozen by the arthritis into
crooked claws. Her fingers were at a
forty-five degree angle to her hands.

Our nurse gently lifted her onto a
bedpan, and then wound the call light around
her hands. "Squeeze the pad when you're done," she

murmured to her patient, then left the room.
We followed her to the next room where an
alarm was beeping. Expertly checking

the IV she turned off the alarm and
left to answer the phone at the nurses'
station. "Second floor, Tracy RN," she

said. "But we can't take another admit,"
she argued into the phone. "Both my aide
and my unit secretary are on

"break and I'm here alone…" the arthritic
woman's call light went on. "No I didn't
let them leave together. They've pulled this on

"me before. I can't. If there were someone
else I could call in to help I wouldn't
be working a sixteen hour shift with

"a bad back. Go ahead and call in the
nursing supervisor. I need her here
anyway to help with the patients and

"talk to my staff. Here they come now after
sneaking off for a thirty minute break."
Tracy hung up the phone and addressed the

two coworkers. "Karen, Mrs. Johnson
in 201 needs to come off the pan.
Sandy, you need to call Admissions and

"ask about that new patient." Sandy said,
"I thought that was your job. You're the RN,
I'm just a pee-on." "Sandy, please just do

"it. I have to change this IV," Tracy
begged, not looking behind her as she went
into the med room. "I need lifting help

"in 201," came Karen's voice over
the walky-talky. Tracy quickly spiked
a new IV bag and sprinted to the

room where the alarm was sounding again.
The supervisor must have arrived then
because we could hear the two aides complain

about Tracy. A man down the hall was
hollering, "Nurse!" Tracy set the IV
pump and left the room to answer the phone

at the desk. Sandy was on the other
line saying, "Well then fix some mac and cheese
for your brother. You know how to do that."

"Second floor, Tracy RN." The nursing
supervisor was motioning to the
nurse that they needed to talk. "Lifting help

"in 201 – PLEASE!" Tracy covered her
right ear so that her left ear could hear the
doctor's orders. Cradling the phone on her

left shoulder, she wrote with her right hand as
quickly as she could. "Honey, I told you
that I have to work until eleven."

The supervisor finally left to help
Karen in 201 and the man's voice
cried out again, "Nurse!" Tracy was able

to hang up the phone, but she couldn't stand
up without grimacing and grabbing her
back. "Nurse!" Doubled over, Tracy flipped a

switch on a console and said, "Mister Beck,
what can I do for you?" The voice on the
intercom snarled, "I've been calling for an

"hour now. I need my damn pain pill!" Still bent
over, Tracy said patiently, "I told
you at six o'clock that I can't get

"you anything until eight. The doctor
wants you to cut back on the narcotics..."
"I don't care what the damn doctor said. Call

"him up and tell him I'm in pain and I
can't stand it anymore!" Tracy snapped off
the intercom. The supervisor's phone

went off and with hand signals she said she
had to leave. Tracy grabbed the phone again
and with more hand signals begged her to stay.

"Second floor, Tracy RN. Can you hold
for a second?" Without waiting for a
reply Tracy hit the HOLD button and

asked Sandy, "Can you get the other line?"
"I'm already on line three with Helen
from Admissions, remember?" And again

the man's voice yelled "Nurse!" Karen emerged with
an armful of dirty bedding, scowling.
Dante felt along the wall for something.

He snatched my arm - the sinkhole reappeared.

Canto XXVI

back in the sinkhole, on Good vs. Evil

The sinkhole was almost a nice respite
from the chaos we'd just experienced.
But my anger raged at everything I'd

seen. "Those two aides should be fired!" I yelled.
My Teacher calmly stated, "They were. Their
life circumstances are complicated.

"In fact, you'd consider their firing to
also be unjust." I probably was
pouting when I blared out, "Well that shooter

"should have been shot!" "He was, remember?" "Well,
he never should have been born," I ranted.
"Why does God allow evil to exist?

"So far everything you've shown me was so
bizarre that I could take it or leave it.
In fact, I don't think any of it was

"real. This was all just some sort of cruel
joke. I mean, biker dudes and all that stuff.
But these are all things I've seen on the news."

My Mentor sat me down on a nearby
chunk of asphalt and waited for me to
calm down. "None of this is real," he said at

last. "This is all just a holographic
image of things that used to be." I stared
at him for a while, then said, "Yeah, right."

"OK," he said. "Let me try a different
approach. You've read the Bible, right?" Nodding,
my nose and eyes started to leak. "You've read

"various creation stories that came
from other traditions?" Choking down
sobs I nodded again. He handed me

a box of hospital tissues. "You know
how Adam and Eve were banished from the
Garden of Eden for eating of the

"Tree of Knowledge?" I blew my nose, ashamed
of my outburst. "But there was also a
Tree of Life, remember? This Tree of Life

"symbol is repeated in art work all
over the world, as if we're longing to
eat from that tree, too. According to the

"Bible, an archangel guarded Eden
to prevent Adam and Eve from going
back." Hiccupping a sob I said, "They both

"were tested by God and they failed the test."
"Actually," Dante said, "they passed the
test." I stared at him, not believing what

he'd said. "It's true," he continued. "They were
the only species living on Earth at
the time that had the courage, intellect

"curiosity and desire to
learn why they were forbidden to eat of
that fruit. They were the only species that

"wanted knowledge badly enough to risk
it all. They were tested the way a child
in the first grade is tested to see if

"he's ready for the second grade. And their
lives became more difficult because the
second grade is more difficult than first grade

"and it's much harder than kindergarten."
I protested, "But Eve was cursed to bear
children in pain and neither was allowed

"back into Eden!" He nodded, then said,
"Think about evolution. The lower
animals have some discomfort while they

"give birth, but not as much as humans do
because their offsprings' heads are smaller. Our
babies' heads are large enough to hold some

"of that knowledge gained in the Garden of
Eden, with lots of room to spare. And
of *course* the angel kept Adam and Eve

"from returning to Eden! When you were
a child you weren't allowed back into a
kindergarten room once you made it to

"the second grade, and the third and the fourth."
"That still doesn't explain why there's evil,"
I pouted, my nose still running. "We'll get

"there," he explained. "Be patient. The reason
why evil exists is because evil
does not really exist. Remember that

"God created the Heavens and the Earth
in six days?" "Seven," I corrected. "Six,"
he corrected back. "God rested on the

"seventh day. He stepped back, the way parents
step back when their toddler starts to walk. If
they don't, the baby cannot learn this skill."

"I don't get it yet," I complained. He said
patiently, "It's bad when the toddler falls
and gets hurt, right?" I nodded. "And it's bad

"when the child gets sick because he's not in
the germ-free womb anymore, right?" Again
I nodded. "But eventually the

"child learns to walk and hopefully he gets
immunity to whatever made him
sick." "And sometimes the child dies," I argued.

Dante's response — "Then the child is given
another chance to reincarnate if
that is what his soul wants. Perhaps his next

"body will be stronger. Evolution
is part of Creation in the next world,
too. And it's evil," Dante stated, "when

"a deer loses her fawn to a cougar.
And you can say it is evil when an
epidemic wipes out populations.

"And you can say earthquakes and tornadoes
that level cities and kill a lot of
people are evil, right?" "Of course!" I said.

Then came the Socratic zinger. "Are these
events evil, or are they just things that
we haven't learned to control yet. 'And God

"gave dominion to man over the beasts
of the Earth..' Remember that verse?" "Yes," I
answered. He said, "Isn't that like saying

"we have permission to make changes in
our environment?" "Yeah," I held, "and we've
completely messed it up!" Stated Dante,

"We stumble, like a toddler stumbles when
learning to walk. If we are ever to
become co-creators with God we have

"to go through that stumbling and getting back up
and stumbling again." My attention was
aroused. "What do you mean, 'co-creators'?"

His eyes studied me carefully. "I mean
just that. Ponder the multiverse and all
its complexity and beauty. There is

"a lot to learn before we can create
our own universes with evolving
creatures. We'll experiment with physics

"and math to see which natural laws work.
Then we'll return to our Original
Creator to renew and to share what…"

"Enough!" I yelled and ran into a hole.

Canto XXVII

war

I stumbled onto a scene from old news
clips of Vietnam — helicopters dropped
from the sky to pick up wounded, bleeding

nineteen-year-old boys, then flew off amid
crackling gunfire. I saw the same scene
again and then again at newer wars

that the press was no longer allowed to
film. "Get down you idiot! You'll draw fire!"
Immediately I dropped down and looked

for Dante. He was nowhere to be seen.
"Oh, God," I whispered, "I never should have
run away from him." Uncontrollable

shaking possessed my body. I slowly
arose. The soldier who yelled at me had
run off somewhere, leaving me confused and

alone in a baffling time-warp of war
scenarios from different epochs
in history. Superimposed

on modern battles were chariots drawn
by horses, tanks next to centurions
and stealth planes being brought down with arrows.

I walked through battlefields with stricken men
and fighting men and screaming, yelling men.
And frightened men and angry men and dead.

The battlefields were strewn with corpses and
the crawling anguish of those not yet dead.
The bloody togas, spears and M-16's.

The dying horses, burning tanks and bombs –
the broken chariots the putrid black
gunpowder residue and burning flesh.

A trumpet blast, a huge 'hurrah!' a scream,
a silence too deafening to hear,
a canon flash, a cloud of smoke, a thud.

A field of banners, flags and battle shrouds.
Grass crowns, feathers, leather shields and helmets.
Swords and maces brought by helicopters.

Desolation of a once lush mountain,
mountain is rebuilt, replanted, regrown
and desolation comes again later.

When boundaries are redrawn, redefined
when enemies are now allied in blood
and allies become bitter enemies.

When young men, aged in battle, have survived
and lived to make more young men who become
the fathers of more soldiers young and strong

then beaten down by war until their sons
march proudly through their fathers' tearful sighs -
some will live to beget another war.

Time flips forward – backward – forward again.
A farmer's field stripped bare to feed the troops
and oil fields plundered to feed the voters.

And always the widows and orphans starve.
They're guilty only of having been born.
Sometimes birth is caused by rape, sometimes love.

God is on our side God is on our side
such courage and terror and betrayal
and nobility over and over.

Civil war surgeons amputating limbs
Florence Nightingale in the Crimea
MASH units, donkey carts carrying dead.

"Clean the battlefield to prevent disease,"
comes the order from the generals. So
bodies piled high, like firewood, burn.

And the children, the children, the children
always the children – orphaned, running scared,
wounded, starving or street-smart survivors.

Sex slaves, young boys captured and trained to kill.
Stepping on land mines from another war
growing up by themselves, wanting revenge.

Scorched Earth policies, defoliation
Agent Orange poisoning coming back home.
Sherman's march to the sea, burned villages.

Smoking ruins of cities, carpet bombing.
Choking soldiers blinded by mustard gas.
Death camps, prison camps, Holocaust inmates.

Propaganda, rallies and cries for peace.
Refugees, snipers, Cossacks on horseback
terrorizing peasants and stealing crops.

Hun invaders, contract soldiers killing
for the highest bid. Loyal to the Crown
loyal to themselves loyal to bloodshed.

Politicians, generals hide behind
the scene. Taxpayers, tax-takers building
better siege machines airplanes battleships.

Always wanting more. More territory
more riches, more spoils, more bodies floating
down a river which has been stained with blood.

I heard Dante's words, "Pray and discern the
truth." I looked for him again. He wasn't
there. I dropped to the ground and prayed, "Help me!"

Then a blinding light, brighter than the Sun.

The Purgatorio 2.0

Canto I

waking up in Purgatory

My ears still rang from the atomic blast
when I awoke on the beautiful bank
of a river on a pleasant warm day.

A cooling breeze and fragrant flowers soothed
my battered nerves while birds sang healing songs.
Dante was sitting under a large oak.

He held a magazine sideways, scanning
the centerfold. "Where are we?" I asked and
sat up stiffly. "Purgatory," he said.

Then looking at me he asked if I was
OK. I inhaled the scenery and
felt a sense of peace I hadn't known for

what seemed a lifetime. After awhile
I assured my Mentor that I was all
right and commented, "We must have gotten

"separated." "Yup. Sorry about that."
I got up and strolled toward the peaceful
river when suddenly something caught my

eye. "Dante! It's a demon!" He looked up
and said, "Yeah. That's Hector. He likes to
steal things. If he wasn't so gosh darn cute

"I'd chase him away. He's really kind of
a nuisance" The little black creature ran
behind another bush, obviously

stalking us. Dante slowly folded the
magazine and set in on the ground. Then
he took off his robe, revealing jeans and

a plain tee shirt, stretched luxuriously
with a loud yawn and settled back against
the tree. The little demon scurried from

one bush to the other, apparently
eyeing Dante's centerfold. Stuffing his
rolled up robe behind his back to cushion

the solid tree trunk, he clasped his fingers
behind his head and settled back. Turning
his face toward me he winked and gestured

me to be quiet. Sure enough, a black
blur whisked the magazine away to some
hiding place in the bushes. "As soon as

"Hector finds out it's just a *Feline Lover's
Monthly* and the centerfold is a white
Persian cat he'll…" but an angry squeal from

the bushes interrupted Dante. My
Master chuckled merrily, "Serves you right,
Hector!" We both laughed and it felt so nice.

After a while, though, anxious feelings rose
in my gut. "So what do we do now?" I
asked. He shrugged casually and replied,

"I don't know. Rest up a bit." Hector popped
out of the bushes long enough to tell
us in his little-demon chatter just

what he thought of Dante's prank, then scampered
away again. I still worried about
what was going to happen next. "Did you

"get your map back?" I asked, hoping I could
engage him in a little more chit-chat.
"Don't need it any more. Purgatory's

"renovation is complete. Pretty nice
here, don't you think?" "Yes-s-s," I began, "but I
can't help thinking that there's something more we

"should be doing." He finally stood up
and smiled. "That's the Purgatory spirit!
Salvation with something missing. You caught

"on to that one quickly —good work." Just then
I heard a ringtone. I started to ask him
how long he'd had the cell phone but instead

listened to the conversation. "Virgil!"
my Leader exclaimed. "Good to hear from you!"
A long silence followed. I watched his face

turn somber, then he said, "We both made it
out all right." "She seemed a bit shaken, but there
were no injuries." "I know." "I'm sorry."

Still talking into the phone he said, "I
understand, Virgil." "I know and it won't
happen again." "I'm really sorry." "I

know." "I understand." "From now on I'll keep
my personal demons under control."
"Yes, sir." "Good bye." Clicking off the phone he

turned away. Just then Hector trotted up
to Dante and sat in front of him with
an expectant gaze in his beady eyes.

"Hector, get out of here!" Dante shouted.
The little critter backed away a few
feet, then turned and glanced over his right

wing to see what Dante was going to
do next. He sat again, his wings flapping
slowly in anticipation. "GET OUT!"

Cowering low, Hector's snaky tail
formed a question mark and his eyes never
strayed from Dante. My Master ran up to

Hector and chased him as far as the bank
of the river. When Dante turned to leave,
Hector followed at a safe distance and

sat again in a submissive posture.
Suddenly Dante ran up to Hector
and kicked him like a football across

the river, eliciting a sharp yelp
from the creature. Hector disappeared some
where on the opposite shore. Dante hung

his head and stood silently next to the
flowing water until Virgil appeared,
seemingly out of nowhere. I watched the

two from my vantage point several feet
away. Like a coach comforting one of
his players, Virgil placed his arm around

Dante's shoulder and gave him a playful
cuff to the back of his head. Dante seemed
to perk up and returned to where I was.

Cautiously I said, "It looked like Virgil
really yelled at you on the phone." Dante
shrugged. "Everything's fine. Don't worry." I said,

"Maybe Virgil will let you have a dog."

Canto II

intro to Purgatory, Virgil gives Dante a furlough

Dante found a couple of logs for us
to sit on, then facing me he told me,
"I owe you a heartfelt apology

"for letting Hector steal that map. I was
entrusted with your safety and because
we had to stumble around those last few

"rings of Hell without proper directions
I exposed you to unnecessary
harm." I immediately touched his hand

and told him there was nothing to forgive,
but he shook his head and insisted, "I
should have banished Hector long before we

started this journey. Pet peeves and inner
demons have no place in the lives of those
who are seeking the righteous path. The fact

"that my own inner demon — loneliness—
presented in the form of a playful
pet devil attests to the deception

"we can fall victim to when we allow
our neuroses to go unexamined.
That is one of our Purgatory tasks —

"to examine whatever defects in
character can hit us unawares and
banish them without a second thought." He

looked wistfully toward the river. "You
really miss him, don't you?" I remarked. My
Mentor answered, "He reminded me of

"a dog I used to have named Hector. He
was there for me when Beatrice died and
as an old grey-muzzled friend he stayed with

"me when I was exiled from my home town —
from my beloved Florence — where all my friends
and family lived. Virgil is working

"with me on forgiving the Ghibellines
and forging new relationships. This is
my weak spot, and an evil entity

"took advantage of it when trying to
distract us from our spiritual path."
Then shrugging his shoulders as if shaking

off a bad memory, he cheerfully
told me, "Well, let me give you an intro
to Purgatory. They kept some of the

"original features, like the mountain
which is climbed by the pilgrims that leads to
Paradise. Mostly the changes were made

"in the curriculum. Right now we are
in a receiving area. There's a
lot more than you see here. Right around this

"clump of trees is where the souls who just crossed
over are greeted by family and
friends and animals who passed before them."

"Animals?" I asked. Smiling broadly he
shared, "Yes, all animals go to either
Purgatory or Heaven, whichever

"the animal chooses. It can also
choose to reincarnate as either its
former species or as something else. Some

"animals, usually pets, want to
become human. They, too, are souls and are
on a spiritual path leading to

"the Heavenly realms." Dante looked wistful
again. Just then, Virgil appeared. I got
up and asked if they wanted me to leave.

Virgil's voice was a melodious bass.
"No, certainly not, my Child. I'm just here
to accompany you two around that

"bend and to give my friend Dante here a
short break." Dante's face lit up, then Virgil
told him, "Go on! Say 'hi' to everyone."

Like a little boy Dante ran to that
grove he had pointed out before.
Virgil remarked, "The journey through Hell is

"exhausting. We often give each other
some time off. Now if you would like you can
follow me and I will explain things as

"we go along." Virgil chose to remain
in his traditional ancient clothing,
and his long robe caught a fresh, pleasant breeze.

"As you can see," the deep voice proceeded,
"we are at the foot of a mountain." I
looked up and tried to see the summit, but

it was hidden by clouds which floated in
a bright blue sky. It occurred to me that
while in Hell, I could not tell what time of

day it was due to the uniformly
murky grey sky. Virgil remarked, "No, Child.
You cannot see the summit yet. That is

"for those who have completed the steps." "What
steps?" I asked. "You'll see eventually.
Meanwhile, you've seen the upper branch of the

"River Styx." He pointed back to where we
had started. "Those who enter here by the
back way – by way of Hell – must be washed in

"the River to remove the stain of Hell.
Our friend Dante and I took care of that
for you." Reflexively I clenched my shirt

closer to me. A soft bass chuckle, then,
"We arranged for an all-female band of
angels to cleanse you while Dante and I

"went elsewhere to discuss the politics
of fourteenth century Italy. He's
still a bit fixated on that." "Yeah, I

"noticed." Then Virgil pointed to a large
crowd of spirits in the distance who were
laughing and hugging each other. Some had

tears of joy as they embraced loved ones they
obviously missed dearly. I thought I
could see Dante surrounded by a lot

of men and women in Medieval dress.
A large fluffy black dog bounced around my
Mentor. When I asked, Virgil responded,

"Yes, Dante is allowed to have a dog."

Canto III

family reunion

Virgil and I walked past Dante and his
crowd of family and friends, allowing
him his time for joyful reunions.

Virgil said to me, "There are some people
waiting to greet you, too." Apprehension
started to take over my consciousness.

Cheerfully I answered him, "Oh, that's all
right. I mean, I'm glad they all made it here
instead of—you know." "Don't you want to see

"your departed family and friends?" he
asked. "Um, sure," I lied. "It's just that we have
so much to see. I assume we have to

"climb the mountain. At least that's what was in
the *Divine Comedy*. If I recall
correctly…" "Stop changing the subject," he

chided gently. "You may be pleasantly
surprised." "Or not," I muttered. "We really
need to get going, don't we? Is Dante

"coming back or are you going to lead
me?" With a gentle smile Virgil took
my arm and led me to another group

of spirits off to the right. They hadn't
seen me yet so I backed away from him
and offered, "It really looks like a long

"journey and don't we have some sort of time
limit?" "Come on," Virgil said a bit more
assertively. "This is actually

an important part of your mission here.
You can work on reconciliation
now, while you are still alive and can enjoy

"the benefit you will have with other
relationships you currently endure,
or you can meet everybody when you

"die. You won't have as much control over
the situation then. Consider this
opportunity to be a gift." His

gaze was gentle but determined and he
offered me his arm again. "I will be
there with you for support. I promise." I

glanced at Virgil, then I looked over at
the familiar faces which approached
us with the same unease I felt. Two of

my close friends were the first to run up to
me and try to hug me with their spectral
arms. "Sarah!" exclaimed Mary, "you are still

"alive! What's going on?" Virgil told her
that I was invited to explore the
afterlife by special dispensation.

Judy also tried to hug me and said,
"Either way, we are so glad to see you
again. Did you get into some trouble

"or something?" Once more Virgil answered her,
"The prayers of someone who loves her very
much expressed concern for her direction

"in life. Sarah? Don't you want to greet your
old friends?" Tears ran down my cheeks as I said,
"Mary, I feel awful that I didn't

"respond to your last letter. I didn't
know what to say when you told me about
the cancer. I wish I had been there for

"you. Judy, you died so young. What did you
die of? I keep dreaming about you and
in my dream you are a single mom with

"three kids and I see a pier over a
lake or something. Can you both forgive me
for neglecting our friendship and instead

"pouring all my energy into my
career?" Both of the shades snuggled close to
me and seemed to fill me with love and peace.

Then my father and grandparents joined them.
"Sarah," my grandmother began, "we all love
you so much. You know our family's not

"the huggy type and for some reason the
words 'I love you' are the most difficult
words for our family to say. I thought

"you just knew how precious you are to us."
My father joined in, "I wish I could take
back all the words I *did* say. I wasn't

"mad at you. I was still so nervous from
the war that everything would irritate
me. I could see the hurt in your face when

"I yelled at you and that made me even
madder. I'm so sorry I hurt you. I
wish I could make it up to you somehow…"

More tears streamed down my face as I reached
for him and sobbed, "I'm sorry I failed you.
I'm sorry I left home at eighteen but

"I wish you could understand why I had
to start my life somewhere else. I wasn't
looking for trouble or being wayward.

"I just wanted to go to college and
be free to think and say what I believe
and prepare for a career that allowed

"me to support myself so I wouldn't
need some husband's paychecks." His ghostly tears
flowed as freely as mine when he told me,

"I know I was mean to your mother, too.
It was the war. There was so much that kept
coming back to me. The shelling. I tried

"to talk it out so all of you could see
why I was so tense…" "I love you, Dad!" I
cried as I tried to fall into his arms.

Then one by one aunts and uncles came up
to me and gave me ghostly caresses.
"We were afraid that you were rejecting

"us. None of us went to college and we
were afraid that maybe you were ashamed
of us." The words burst from my heart, "No! I

"could never be ashamed of any of
you! You were the ones who taught me how to
work hard and live the best life I could live!"

"And we never told you how proud we are."

Canto IV

the Family Interview

Soon I was busy catching up with all
those family I had known years ago.
I didn't even realize how much

I had loved them and missed them. I received
a live – so to speak – genealogy
that went back centuries as ancestors

came forward to introduce themselves and
to tell me their stories. I learned about
life in the 1700's and the

1600's and earlier. There were
a lot of farmers, of course, but also
blacksmiths, one sailing merchant who added

some exotic genes to my DNA,
one lady-in-waiting to some French queen
and a lot of soldiers from different

eras. Several of my beloved
pets came up to me wagging their tails and
purring. There was even one chipmunk I

had befriended on a camping trip.
For some reason I could feel their sloppy
noses and tongues slobbering all over

my face and I could once again bury
my fingers in their luxurious fur.
I asked one of my great aunts, "I didn't

"know until today that animals can
get to Heaven. I'm so happy to know
that!" She stroked the fur of my grey Persian

cat and replied, "These dogs, cats and other
animals are such pure spirits that they
do not sin," she snuggled Smokey, "even

"when they destroy the house in their unique
little ways. My own collie and I talked
about..." "You talked to your dog?" I asked her.

"Oh, yes. There are a lot of barriers
broken down around here," she responded.
"Where is your collie?" I asked. "Well that's what

"we talked about. Shep decided that he
wanted to reincarnate on Earth. He
wanted to try being a human this time.

"I still watch over him from here. He's quite
the dandy, as you might expect from a
gorgeous dog like he was." She shook her head.

"I just hope he doesn't go overboard
with the ladies while he's down there. He is
acquiring some bad Karma." Then

I felt a familiar hand on my
shoulder. "Have you had enough visiting?"
Dante asked. Without thinking I tried to

hug him but his body was now spectral.
"Why?" I started to ask, but he answered
me with, "I'll explain later. There is still

"some daylight left and we need to cover
more ground before nightfall." I waved goodbye
to my friends, pets and family — some of

whom I had just met. They all smiled and
reassured me that we would meet again.
"Dante, why couldn't I feel any of

"them and why are you sometimes solid and
sometimes ghostly?" We walked past many more
spirit groups as we slowly approached the

foot of the mountain. "Some of them," he said,
"have not progressed far enough through the Steps
and others choose not to have physical

"contact at that time. I solidify
when there is a need for it. When you tried
to hug me just now it would have been too

"distracting for you. Once again you need
to focus on your Astral body in
order to complete the next part of your

"journey. And congratulations on your
Family Interview. Virgil stepped in
because he and I both knew you needed

"a firmer approach before you would be
willing to take that leap." My thoughts bounded
through my head at a dizzying rhythm.

"Dante, I thought Hell was overwhelming
but now I'm even more unsure about
everything." "That's why I brought you away

"from those emotional reunions.
It's time now to rest while I explain
what's next on the agenda." We found a

comfortable spot in a lovely
grove of oaks. The sun was beginning to
set and showed off its brilliant red hues.

Dante pointed to an area in
front of us and a crackling bonfire
appeared. "How did you do that?" I gasped. He

flashed a nonchalant grin and said, "It's not
important. You'll understand later on."
Suddenly I realized that time had

passed and I had not eaten. I wasn't
hungry either. "Dante? How long have we
been on this journey?" "Friday, Saturday

"and today is Easter Sunday. Just like
it was when Virgil led me on my path."
I exclaimed, "Three days and I'm not hungry?!"

"The Grace of God is nourishment enough
for Man, beast, insect, bird or fish or plant.
Even the souls of plants are honored here,"

he told me. I blurted out, "Oh my God,
I've eaten animals with souls and plants
which are also alive." He chastised me

with, "Do not call upon the Divine One
unless you are praising It or are in
immediate need of something." My heart

sank as I answered him, "I seem to be
messing up every moment I live. I
can't help but – you know – sin. I don't know what

"to do or where I can turn." Again
a smile crossed his face. "You are breezing
through your Program! You've just completed your

"First Step, 'admitted we were powerless
over sin and our spirits had become
unmanageable'. Good work!" He told me.

"Now rest. Tomorrow we will start early."

Canto V

the resting place

I awoke refreshed when rosy-fingered
dawn appeared at the horizon. "We don't
plagiarize Homer around here," my

Teacher scolded me. "Sorry, I couldn't
resist the urge." I teased. "Has any of
this spiritual quest seemed like something

"to joke about?" His sudden harshness took
me by surprise. "You have been given a
gift and you need to show proper respect."

We both rose to our feet wordlessly and
proceeded along a narrow path that
led to an open meadow. Hundreds of

souls lounged and chatted within such pleasant
surroundings as I had never seen. Not
only did lush trees and a babbling brook

answer to the delightful songs of birds,
but when he did choose to speak again my
Guide informed me that the climate always

remained pleasant and the bountiful plant
life somehow stayed fresh without rain or storms.
"This part of the multiverse," he said, "is

"a place of rest and renewal for those
whose lives on Earth were filled with hardship and
misery. These virtuous spirits are

"given anything they desire. A
few souls down the way crave the bright city
lights with shopping districts, entertainment

"and the like. These here are nature lovers.
Shades who crave solitude have their own rests.
They even have a Valhalla where some

"spirits can fight, wrestle and compete with
each other, just as their own folklore had
promised. Spirits who are tormented by

"horrible memories are instantly
comforted by their guardian angels.
And spirits who were unsuccessful in

"life with their battles against various
addictions have continuous contact
with their angels until a care plan can

"be agreed upon." I asked him, "How long
are spirits allowed to stay here?" He said,
"As long as their healing process requires."

"I'd stay here forever," I chimed, drinking
in the sunshine and the fresh, cooling breeze.
Dante nodded in agreement but said,

"The consciousness longs for experience.
Although they've suffered greatly and worked hard
in life, someday they'll find a need for growth.

"Sedentary rest is not a normal
condition of the mind. Inquisitive
and adventurous, the mind yearns to grow."

I added, "Idle hands are the Devil's
workshop." "And what do you mean by that?" he
asked. "Well," I pondered, "it seems like boredom

"is the cause of a lot of transgressions."
"A wise observation," he agreed. "Tell
me more." "I guess I'm thinking about a

"teenager who steals a car for thrills, or
a married couple who cheat, or someone
who drinks or gambles because of boredom."

"These are the old souls," Dante remarked, "who
have been through many incarnations
over hundreds, sometimes thousands of years.

"When they return to the Reception Place
their memories come back of previous
lives where they had debauched. Most of them lose

"their desire for mischief, therefore, while
they are here." "I'm confused again," I said.
"What is the difference between getting

"reborn on Earth and climbing the mountain
of Purgatory as you described in
the *Divine Comedy*?" My Beloved

Mentor responded, "Purgatory is
kind of a fast-track into Paradise
and as such it is much more challenging.

"Some spirits believe they can gain merit
by reliving a mortal existence
on Earth or some other planet. Also

"there are soul groupings who are so attached
to each other that they cannot bear to
be separated, should one progress more

"rapidly on the mountain than its mates.
These soul groupings are the ones who are sons
in one lifetime, then parents of their parents

"the next lifetime, then lovers or soulmates.
On Earth, for example, these soul groups tend
to manifest as close-knit families

"or as inseparable friends. Life on
Earth can involve a lot of suffering,
but it can also continue rather

"pleasantly for lifetime after lifetime.
Sometimes the guardian angels have to
allow some tragedy into a life

"to push it out of its complacency
and encourage it to seek the Pathway
again." "That sounds rather mean," I complained.

"A lot of things will seem cruel until
you see the complete picture," he stated.
"Is Purgatory really that bad?" I

asked him. He shrugged a bit. "I wouldn't call
it bad. It's more like a combination
of boot camp, drug treatment and doctoral

"dissertation. One's guardian angel
accompanies the evolving soul through
all the Steps until completion allows

"entry into Paradise." "You keep talking
about Steps like this is some sort of twelve
step program." "Actually," he said, "it

"is. Jesus tried to teach the program and
not only was he crucified, but all
of those gospels were burned when Constantine

"unified all of the Christian sects
at Nicea. The Buddha was able
to have his Eightfold Path accepted by

a great many people in the East.
But then elsewhere a few others also
were inspired to teach it and were not

"accepted. Finally in Ohio
two men shared their inspiration and were
able to apply it to addiction

"recovery." "Thank God for that!" I said.

Canto VI

a fork in the road

We didn't have far to travel before
we reached a fork in the road. Dante turned
to me and said, "Well, here it is." I asked

him what he was talking about. "This is
where the spirit decides whether to be
reborn or to work its Steps on the Mount

"of Purgatory." I looked around a
large boulder and saw a path leading off
to the right. It was marked by a sign that

said, 'Welcome to Purgatory. Watch your
step'. "Somehow I expected a greeting
that's a bit more poetic," I grumbled.

"Whatever," sighed Dante, rolling his eyes.
"Anyway we're going to travel straight
ahead on this path, look around and

"then double back to this fork again." He
didn't waste any time following the
trail to another huge Reception Place.

Everybody was grouped in pairs. I
asked him why that was and he said, "All the
souls you've met are accompanied by their

"guardian angels. The angels just weren't
visible to you back there." "Why?" "Because
in this receiving area they have

"to be absolutely sure that their shade
is seeing and hearing everything they
say. This is where important decisions

"are being made and instructions given.
This process can sometimes take several
Earth months as the angel and its shade make

"decisions about which planet the soul
will incarnate on, which life goals they need
to formulate and who the soul's parents

"will be." "Do you mean we choose our parents?"
"For the most part, yes. Sometimes there are flaws,
like when two or more souls compete for the

"same set of parents, or when two or more
couples are having sex near each other
and the soul falls into the wrong couple."

Noting my disgusted facial grimace
he added, "We're not always dealing with
kinky group sex scenes. Apartment buildings

"after a World Cup tournament conceive
quite a few babies in a short time span.
Ask any OB nurse about snow storms,

"championship games, bikini weather
and holidays. My own kids were conceived
during holidays because that was the

"only time Gemma could get drunk enough
to have sex with me. It was an arranged
marriage, you see." I could also see that

he was ugly enough to pose for a
cathedral's gargoyle statue, but I
chose to say instead," I'm sorry to hear

"that." He thanked me for the sentiment then
added, "The kids all looked like Gemma. God
is merciful." "Oh, Dante," I reproached

"have you ever considered getting rid
of that stupid looking stocking cap with
the ear flaps and wearing a cowboy hat

"instead? It would match your new jeans better."
He thought about it for a moment then
looked around as if remembering our

mission. "Now what was I talking about?"
he mused. "Sex." "No, before that." "Choosing our
parents. " "Oh, yeah," he said, "thanks. Now our sense

"of judgement isn't necessarily
better here than it is when we're alive.
Sometimes our potential mothers don't want

"us and we are either aborted or
otherwise shunned, and sometimes the mother's
uterus cannot carry a baby

"to term. In both cases there is a grief
process which has to be dealt with. On this
end the guardian angels spend a lot

"of time working with their shades to help them
overcome feelings of abandonment
or grief and encourage the souls to look

"for another mother. And souls looking
for a certain father pose another
challenge. Women, as you know, produce just

"one egg per month, but latching onto all
those millions of sperm is tricky, to
say the least. They usually tell the

"soul to wait until their potential dad
reincarnates as a woman." Dante
looked distracted again. "Then what?" I asked.

"Then what — what?" I smirked at his discomfort,
"What happens after the egg and sperm unite?"
"Oh, really," Dante said, rolling his eyes,

"didn't your mother have this talk with you?"
"Dante, what is the next step before a
soul reincarnates. Now come on. You can

"get through this sex stuff. Just focus," I laughed.
"Whatever. OK," he said. "The spirit
and its angel get in that line you see

"over there," he pointed, "and they wait their
turn to get shrunken." "Huh?" "Yes, the spirit
has to shrink to embryo size, then its

"angel carefully carries the baby
to its chosen couple and it becomes
a fetus." I laughed again. "What?" he asked.

"So *that* is where that stork idea came from!"

Canto VII

back to the gate of Purgatory

With the line of babies being dispatched
merrily to their new parents and with
Dante cooling off to a cold splash of

water, our journey recommenced back to
the gate of Purgatory. My Leader
inserviced me on the protocol for

addressing the angel who guards the gate.
"Now remember," he said, "attitude is
everything. The angel really expects

"humility, piety and a true
desire to repent and change your ways.
Do you think you can carry that one off?"

"Oh, really," I told him, rolling my eyes.
He gave me a sideways glance then said,
"After you prostrate yourself before the

"angel, he will carve seven P's in your
forehead…" "He will do no such thing!" I yelled.
Dante gave me another dirty look

and said, "As you go up the mountain and
properly repent of the seven sins
the P's will be removed one by one." "They'll

"leave a scar." "No they won't." We reached the gate
just then. A huge angel towered over
us. I felt a natural instinct to

lay down in front of the angel and beg
for forgiveness. He was a very big
angel. Apparently satisfied, he

let us through the gate and a huge choir
of angels sang 'hallelujah'. "Nice touch,
hey?" Dante mused, admiring the music.

We had a long and torturous path to
climb to get to the first level. The sides
of the path were accompanied by signs

that read, 'No swearing', 'No spitting', 'No drugs
or alcohol', 'No weapons', 'Keep off the
grass', 'Keep off the other grass too', 'No sex'

'No thinking about sex', 'No talking', 'No
cameras', 'No texting', 'No shirt-No shoes-
No service', 'Do not remove tag under

'penalty of law', and 'Whatever you
are thinking of doing, don't even think
about it'. I whispered to Dante, "How

"can I remember all of these?" "They have
church ladies," he whispered back, "stationed at
checkpoints along the way who remind you."

A harsh "S-S-S-H-H-H" came from three directions at
once. My Master and I crept silently
forward until we reached a large clearing.

Reaching up to my forehead I could feel
an actual imprint of seven P's!
All I could think about was the plastic

surgery I would need whenever — or
if ever — I could see my beloved
home again. "Dante?" I whispered, "just how

"weird does my forehead look?" A chorus of
church ladies hissed their sharp "S-S-S-H-H-H!" from many
locations near and around us. I snuck

in a quickly whispered, "What does the 'P' stand
for?" A gentle angel stepped in front of
us and answered in a voice so sweet and

kind, "Peccatum is Latin for sin. It
wasn't so very long ago that they
erased a P from your own blessed Guide's:

"forehead." Dante bowed low while pushing me
down to do the same. The angel motioned
for us both to arise then said, "It's truly

"sad that your manuscript was so badly
altered. I know that you tried to portray
your journey as accurately as you

"could." To me the angel said, "Torments here,
per the *Comedy*, sound like punishments
from Hell. But the goals are to educate,

"cleanse the soul and to build the skills which are
needed to progress further along this
path. Let me introduce you to other

"pilgrims." We walked toward a gathering
of souls who stared at me, as if in shock.
Instinctively I pushed my hair over

my forehead to hide the marks. Laughing, the
angel said, "They're staring at your shadow.
See? They all have the same marks on their heads."

Sure enough, the entire assembly
was full of P's and it was now my turn
to stare. Addressing now the multitude

of souls, the angel announced, "Yes, she is
alive. She's here on a special journey,
accompanied by Dante and Virgil."

Several spirits pressed forward to greet
me and to introduce themselves. Just as
in the original *Comedy*, a

few ghosts asked me to send a message to
a loved one who was still alive on Earth.
Turning to Dante and to the angel

I asked if there was anything I could
write with so I could record their requests.
"Don't worry about it," the angel said

pushing me ahead. "They'll find other ways
to communicate. They haven't learned yet
how to enter someone else's dreams. For

"now let's go to the main learning center.
You've probably already heard about
the Steps." I nodded. The angel resumed,

"Well, the tutoring here is more of a
continuum than it is discrete steps.
The paths to enlightenment were revealed

"to several individuals at
different times and they all added their
own interpretations. The cornices

"described in the *Purgatorio* are
just one way to assess the progress of
each Pilgrim." "Does that mean these P's on my

"forehead aren't really necessary?" I
asked. Dante and the angel glanced at each
other. Dante said, "They seem to be more

"of a distraction than a learning tool."
The angel swept a wing across my face,
apparently erasing them, then said,

"Pride is already getting in your way."

Canto VIII

pride, the Angel of Pride

I know my voice was whiney again when
I turned to them both and said, "I am still
powerless over sin. I thought I was

"over that. Don't you remember, Dante?
Before we went through the gate I said I
was powerless over sin and you said

"I was breezing through the steps." My Teacher
glanced back at the angel and with a sad
smile said, "Admitting powerlessness

"is just the first step toward beginning
a process. It is so important to
change our focus from being the center

"of the universe to realizing
that we are only a part of it and
we need all of the other parts if we

"are to become whole." The angel handed
me a handkerchief and added, "It is
normal to backslide into believing

"that we either can, or should, totally
be in control of everything around
us. Powerlessness is a frightening

"feeling. It feels like we're treading water
in the middle of a huge ocean with
no rescue in sight." I sniffed out the

words, "But how can we live like this — knowing
that we're not in control of anything?"
The angel swept me up in his wings and

told me to look around. We were high in
the air looking down on a rapidly
shrinking mountain. Dante was a speck, then

disappeared entirely, then he joined
us in the air, hanging on to his new
cowboy hat that actually looked quite nice.

The angel's voice (the angel himself was
no longer in sight, leaving me hanging
in the air next to Dante) said, "Can you

"see what admitting your powerlessness
can accomplish? By plugging into the
resources around you, you can achieve

"so much more than is possible to do
on your own." I panicked and grabbed for
Dante again, as I had so many

times before. Like Jesus grabbing the arms
of his disciple — who almost believed
that he, too, could walk on water — Dante

took my hands. He and the angel rested
me gently back onto the solid ground.
My angel reappeared and asked, "What have

"you learned from this exercise?" "I learned that
my entire existence depends on
one crazy angel and a ghost." Then I

remembered where I was and who I had
to suck up to in order to return
home. "I mean, you know, no disrespect, but

"the two of you scared the living daylights
out of me!" Dante said to the angel,
"Her adrenaline sometimes blocks up her

"higher thought processes." "I noticed that."
Then turning back toward me the angel
said, "We're both sorry for frightening you

"but we did get your attention. Now think
about why you reached for my friend, Dante,
over here." I didn't even need to

formulate my response. "Because he has
saved me before and I knew he could save
me again." My Beloved Guide chimed in

"Kind of like God, hey?" Noting my turmoil
he added. "No, I'm not God, but you have
also been saved before by a Power

"greater than your own and greater than me
or Anandiel here. Do you believe
that?" Eagerly I responded, "Yes! I

"do!" Dante and the angel exchanged a
high-five. "Step one," Dante said, "admitted
we were powerless over everything.

"Step two. Came to believe that a Power
greater than ourselves could save us." "What is
Step three?" I asked eagerly. "Turned our will

"and our lives over to the care of our
Higher Power, asking only for the
knowledge of Its will and the power to

"carry it out," spoke Anandiel. "You
see?" Dante interrupted, "you really
are breezing through the Steps and it is not

"even noon yet." Continuing, "We're not
trying to intimidate you or break your
spirit. We're just trying to show you what

"pride is and how it stands between you and
the purpose God has for you." The three of
us kept walking. I humbly thanked them both.

"Oh, Dante?" I added, "I like your hat."

Canto IX

lecture on sin

We walked into a large outdoor classroom
setting where students casually lounged
in a natural amphitheater.

Anandiel excused himself, leaving
me and Dante to attend the lecture.
Some of the students were informally

sipping what looked like mint juleps. When I
asked my Mentor about it, he said that
it was a soothing ambrosia mix

analogous to herbal tea, with
whatever flavor the student enjoyed
most on Earth. "May I have one?" I asked. "No,"

Master Dante declared. "The beverage
is a potion for the students. Besides,
your mortal body can't handle the drink."

I received the usual stares when my
mortal body cast its shadow again.
By this time I had learned to just smile

wave and sit in the shade of a rock or
tree. Another angel mingled with the
students and made his way to the front of

the group. Dante whispered to me, "Now just
listen, don't contribute, don't ask questions.
Remember that you are just a guest here."

I nodded and sat as humbly as I
could. "The angel is Selathon." I tried
to suppress a giggle, but it came out

my nose. "S-s-s-h-h-h!" Dante hissed, flashing me
an angry look. Whispering fiercely to
me then, "He is a mighty Prince among

"angels and you are here only by a
special dispensation." Once again I
assumed what I believed was a humble

and contrite posture. Fake it 'til you make
it, as they say. The angel began his
lecture with a surprisingly high-pitched

voice. I dug my fingernails into my
hands and bit my lip hard enough to stop
another giggle in its tracks. "What is

"sin?" the angel asked the class. Several
hands shot up, volunteering, "To choose bad
instead of good," "Breaking the commandments,"

and "Disobeying God." It reminded
me so much of my old Sunday school that
I had to bite my lip again. Then the

angel asked them, "What is good and what is
evil?" Many answers were offered, like
"Being nice," "Helping others," "Giving to

"the poor." The angel encouraged more talk
to pour in before he commented, "If
a person steals from the rich to give to

"the poor, is he doing good or is he
doing evil?" Most of the students were
in agreement that the act was a good

one. "But what," the angel continued, "if
the rich person was carrying goods to
be distributed among the poor when

"those goods were robbed?" This stimulated a
lively discussion which I would have liked
to join. "In times of war," he asked anew,

"whose side is God on?" The opinions
ranged from, "It depends which side we are on,"
to, "God is on the side of those who fight

"for the right cause." Selathon roamed between
the students and asked, "How many times do
soldiers choose to fight for a morally

"unjust cause? What if no war is ever
justified?" This time several spirits
indignantly defended honor, the

homeland, defense, "... and pride," the angel said.
Some souls huffed away. "Don't forget conquest,
acquiring resources, all for the good

"of the right people. As a general
rule, we all think we are the ones who are
right, don't we?" Two more spirits abruptly

left the lecture, one of them exclaiming,
"My sons died in battle and yes, they were
fighting to defend our country! For shame!"

The angel continued his lecture with,
"You've seen and heard what pride can lead to, but
you still have not given me a meaning

"of the word 'sin'." He looked around at his
muted students who probably were too
frightened to speak, so instead he professed,

"Some theologians have said that sin is
anything that separates us from God."
I whispered to Dante, "What's going to

"happen to those students who left?" "They'll have to
repeat the lecture," he responded. "There
isn't any room here for politics.

"Believe me," he added, "as passionate
as I was about Florence way back in
1307, I have this lecture

"memorized. So many of my friends and
kinsmen died in those skirmishes because
we knew we were defending the right cause

"but do you remember any of them? Or
even know what the two sides were fighting
for?" I shook my head. "It was pride," he said.

Selathon's squeaky voice lectured on to
the class about how pride can intrude on
our religions. "Some truly virtuous

"people in the world claim there is no such
thing as sin. Is that prideful?" There were mixed
responses from the students. "And there are

"sects that claim there is no afterlife." There
were a few delighted giggles from the
multitude of souls who obviously

were dead, yet alive. Then a few students
suddenly vanished. "Oops," the angel said,
"there go the Taoists. Don't worry. They're

"still around here somewhere, they just fail to
believe it." More chuckles from the students.
"Now along with this series of lectures,"

Selathon said with a flourish of his
wings, "there is some required reading." A
huge library of books, manuscripts, rolls

of parchment and papyrus, clay tablets
and electronic media appeared
out of nowhere. "For those of you who do

"not read Sanskrit, Cuneiform, Persian,
hieroglyphics, Latin, ancient Greek or
Hebrew along with at least three modern

"languages there are translators.
And for those of you who simply cannot
read at all, there are tutors who will be

"available twenty-four seven, three
sixty five – those of you from Earth will please
explain to the others what that means. Take

"as many Earth-centuries as you need."
Dante asked if I wanted to browse, but
I just stared at the massive library.

"OK, then. Let's head to the next stairway."

Canto X

stairway to second cornice, envy

The climb up this next stairway amazed me
because it was much easier, even
though it was just as long and just as steep.

"You wrote about that in your *Comedy*.
Something about how the lighter burden
from less sin made your climb easier. He

sort of grunted, but didn't answer for
awhile. Then he said, "Let me tell you
something about that angel with the queer

"name and the squeaky voice." I knew I was
in trouble again. "Selathon was the
angel who helped Joshua bring down the

"walls of Jericho. Back then he used his
normal speaking voice to say, 'Fall, unclean
city'. These words weren't recorded in the

"Bible because no human ear could hear
them. The trumpet blasts were designed to shield
the ears of the Israelites, or else

"Selathon's voice would have destroyed them, too.
When he lowers the volume then the pitch
of his voice it gets kind of squeaky. When

"he lowers it even more it becomes
subsonic and causes earthquakes. You need
to remember these things and maintain a

"reverence for these angelic beings."
"I'm sorry," I said. He paused in his tracks
and responded, "Not as sorry as you could

"be if you deride any more of the
heavenly host we will meet along the
way." Picking up the pace again, Dante

lectured, "We're coming up to the second
cornice — the envious. My censors wrote
that the sinners' eyes were sewn shut, but God

"is not spiteful like that. The Creator
doesn't torture souls into submission
but rather It teaches and patiently

"waits for the learning process to evolve."
"Hey, Dante? May I ask you a question?"
"You already have. That means you've used up

"your quota for today." He looked over
at me. "I'm kidding. What do you want to
know?" I smiled back and asked, "Why are there

"different cornices for different
sins? I mean, what if a person commits
more than one or two sins in his or her

"lifetime? And why are there only seven
deadly sins? Whatever happened to
the ten commandments? And what if people

"commit sins and then do everything they
can to make amends and repent from those
sins? Do they still have to go through the rings

"of Purgatory? And what if we're not
Catholic? Does that mean Purgatory
doesn't exist for non-Catholics? And

"what if a sin for one culture is a
virtue for another? You know, something
like honor killings or stealing from an

"enemy? What if…" My Teacher cut me
off, "I should have left you with Selathon.
He's the one who asks questions that people

"have struggled with for ages and ages.
I heard that he gives extra credit to
anyone who can prove the existence

"of God and document that proof in
three ancient and two modern scholarly
writings." He paused. "I'm kidding again." "I

"know." The lecture area we came to
this time consisted of scores of students
sitting in front of a Buddha statue.

I carefully ducked from one shadow to
the next and was able to avoid stares
and whispers from the shades. Master Dante

confessed to me, "I've criticized you for
not taking this journey seriously
enough, but I've also been too flippant

"at times, and I apologize. Part of
my responsibility to you is
to serve as a role model and mentor."

Somewhat puzzled, I told him that it
was OK. Then his focus changed and
he said, "On this cornice, the statue starts

"to speak as soon as everyone settles
down and adopts an appropriately
humble, teachable attitude. It's like

"a review of the previous lessons
on Pride, but it's a lab session." We sat
quietly, waiting for the Buddha to

speak. At long last, the statue came to life,
saying, "All people suffer – not just you.
Envy arises when we believe that

"someone else is enjoying life without
paying the same emotional price that
we are. During this lecture we will be

"distributing prayer shawls. Once every one
has a shawl, my assistants will give you
orders to pass your shawl to the person

"on your right. In case of confusion, they
will also take care of the mistakes in
order to keep the shawls circulating.

"When I signal the helpers, you may keep
the shawl you have in your hand at that time."
Several angels passed around plain white

prayer cloths as described. The Buddha statue
then announced, "The Four Noble Truths are — first —
everyone suffers. I have already

"told you this. Second — the root cause of all
suffering is desire. I will teach
you more about that shortly. Third — there is

"the possibility of ending that
suffering. Fourth — the Eightfold Path is the
way to end suffering. There will be more

"on the Eightfold Path also. But for now
I will describe for you the causes of
that desire which leads to suffering."

Then he told them to stop passing the shawls.

Canto XI

prayer shawl exercise, causes of desire, Eightfold Path

At first there was embarrassed chattering
as the students tried to sort out the shawls
among themselves. The Buddha once again

became a statue until the angel
helpers finished handing out the cloths and
settled the students. Reanimated,

the statue came to life again and spoke.
"The purpose of the prayer shawls will become
apparent shortly. Let us return now

"to the causes of envy. First, greed or
desire for something or property
we do not have will cause suffering from

"envy. Next, ignorance or delusion
about someone else due to envy will
cause suffering. Third, envy can create

"hatred and destructive urges, which, of
course, lead to suffering for everyone
involved. Now, I would like you to pick up

"your prayer shawls, which have received energy
from all of the other students present.
If you think about any student here

"and touch the shawl, that student's memories
will appear to you. In that way you will
see that even those souls who were wealthy

"or beautiful, or in some other way
talented had something else in their lives
which made them suffer, just as all of you

"have also suffered. In this way you will
see that envy is a pointless waste of
your spiritual energy." Murmurs

of amazement spread through the crowd, so the
Buddha again froze into his granite
countenance. Dante and I listened to

a couple of nearby spirits who touched
their prayer cloths together as one exclaimed,
"I understand now how Karma drove us

"together for one lifetime after
another. In Egypt I envied you
because you were a scribe and you could give

"your family so much more than I could as
a fisherman." The other spirit
equally excited, confessed, "Do you

"remember when we were brothers in France?
As firstborn I inherited the whole
of our father's estate. I regret that

"I didn't share it with you. If I had
we could have dissolved some Karma instead
of reliving our jealousy over

"and over again." The first spirit then
said, "We were husband and wife in Persia.
If I had ignored what my cohorts told

"me about the proper roles of husbands,
we could have enjoyed our relationship
and our children instead of living as

"two strangers under the same roof." Hugging
each other now, the second spirit said,
"I think we did neutralize some Karma

"in that lifetime because the other wives
told me that they, too, felt envious of
their husbands for their freedom and power.

So it continued as Master Dante
and I strolled amid the shades and listened
to their conversations. Soldiers could now

see that their officers bore a lot of
responsibility and felt lifelong
agony for the deaths of troops. Sons

and daughters understood the pain they caused
their parents in one life, and no longer
felt envy when they themselves became the

parents in the next life. They knew now that
other parents weren't blessed with better kids
or more money to school them better — they

were just experiencing Karma. There
was a lot of hugging and weeping as
souls touched each other's prayer shawls and exchanged

warmest sentiments together. After
awhile the angels encouraged the
spirit-pilgrims to settle quietly

so that Buddha could teach them the Eightfold
Path. Clustered now in pairs and small groups,
the assembled souls waited eagerly

for the statue to reawaken and
share its inspiration. "The Wisdom Path,"
the Buddha resumed, "contains 'Right View' and

"'Right Resolve'. The 'Right View' is seeing the
truth of the afterlife and the effects
of Karma on our reincarnation.

"And what is 'Right Resolve'? Being resolved
on freedom from ill will — on harmlessness.
The Moral Virtues Path is 'Right Speech', 'Right

"Action', and 'Right Livelihood'. We must not
lie, or speak to create discord, or speak
abusively, or engage in idle

"chatter. To achieve 'Right Action' we must
abstain from killing, stealing, sexual
misconduct. This is 'Right Action'. A 'Right

"Livelihood' is one which does no harm to
sentient beings by cheating them or
harming them in any way, such as trade

"in weapons, living beings, meat, poisons
or alcoholic beverages. The
Meditation Path is 'Right Effort', which

"is avoidance of sensual desire,
ill will, doubts about the Eightfold Path, or
drowsiness, or restlessness or any

"other thing that distracts us from the Path.
'Right Mindfulness' is the contemplation
of our feelings, mental states and mental objects

"such as worldly desire and sadness.
And 'Right Concentration' is the detached
state of stillness which is meditation."

Awakening Dante from his dreamlike
rapture at the sound of the Buddha's words
I said sharply, "I hope you realize

"that Buddha didn't recognize women."

Canto XII

the wrathful

Dante said to me on the way to the
next stairway, "OK, you're not Buddhist. So
what are you?" "Homesick," I snapped back, "When do

"I get my ruby red slippers so I
can make a wish and go home?" "You don't like
it there either," Dante snarled. It was

the truth of that remark that stung and left
me with a sudden emptiness. If not
home, then where? Dante broke my insecure

moment, saying, "This is the cornice of
the wrathful. Let's see what's at the top of
these stairs." Still humbled by the upsetting

insight into my own character, I
followed him obediently. Again,
the stairway felt lighter than the other

two. The sun was now lowering into
late afternoon and I was conscious of
my own shadow – but nobody else's –

lengthening. As before I skipped between
trees and rocks trying to hide my mortal
darkness in the shadowed relief they held

for me. Then Anandiel's light appeared
from behind a rock wall and lengthened to
announce the angel's arrival. His light

opposed the light of the setting sun
so that my shadow was neutralized. I
greeted the angel eagerly, as did

Dante. The three of us strode, confident,
to the lecture area and took our place among
the student-pilgrims. Then an angelic

instructor went forward to begin his
discourse. "Greetings, Anandiel. It's good
to see you again." My angel smiled

and nodded a return greeting. "And it's
good to see Dante and your charge." Waiting
for the class to settle, the instructor

began. "Who can tell me what wrath is?" A
few hands went up and answers given
included, "Being angry", "Hating a

"person", "Getting revenge", and "Being pissed
off all the time." The lecturer then asked,
"Is it good or bad to be wrathful?" All

the souls agreed that wrath is bad. "And what
about the Wrath of God?" This question stumped
the group. "All right then. Is there such a thing

"as righteous anger?" Again, the students
hesitated before volunteering
a few answers. "You'll have a chance to talk

"about these things when you break into
your anger management lab groups. You have
all been assigned to various levels

"of anger management depending on
your cantankerousness in life. Those of
you with a very short temper will start

"by reenacting a stubbed toe and work
your way up to road rage, cranky children,
political discussions, catching your

"spouse with a lover, etcetera. Your
guardian angels will direct you to
the proper locations." Anandiel

and Dante chose an area in the shade
to explain the protocols for the wrath
cornice. Dante began, "Most of anger

"is due to pent-up hurts. The goals of this
cornice are to help the pilgrim spirit
uncover and discuss all the causes

"of anger throughout their lives and teach
them coping skills. So, Sarah, what are your
impressions of Purgatory so far?"

"Part of me," I said in a half-whisper,
"is still waiting for everyone to hold
hands and sing Kum Ba Yah near a campfire."

"Oh, Sarah," Dante sighed, "you still have that
stone in your heart that I'd hoped would start to
dissolve by now. Neither fears of Hell nor

"love from Purgatory seem to have touched
that bitter stone yet. When you awaken
from this divinely mandated journey

"you have a chance to change your attitude
while you still live and breathe and walk with
other living people. You could be that

"agent for betterment that you used to
dream about as a child. When did you
forget about your ideals and your hope

"to make a better future? When did you
stop idolizing all those medical
missionaries who devoted their lives

"to serving the poor? When did your love end?"
Anandiel went to greet another
friend while Dante and I walked to the stairs.

Suddenly Dante stopped and hunched over.
"Are you all right?" I cried out, panicked at
his unusual behavior. "I'm fine,"

he growled. "Um, let's take this other route."
"Dante Alighieri!" came a voice
from an obviously irate female

"Where have you been these past three hundred years?!"
"Beatrice, Darling! It's so wonderful
to see you again!" He tried to run

up to her but was blocked by a second
female spirit. "Gemma!" was his awkward
greeting. Spinning his head rapidly back

and forth between the two women he spit
out a greeting, "I've missed both of you so
much…" "Don't give me that crap," snapped Gemma.

"Three or four hundred years - I've lost track — is
a long time to be avoiding me!" "And
me!" exclaimed Beatrice. "And me!" called a

woman across the river. "But after
all," Matilda sighed with a flourish rich
in melodrama, "I have been fated

"to admire you only from afar,
my poet, my darling, my Dante." "Oh
shut up you neurotic banshee!" hollered

Gemma loud enough to be heard across
a river. Beatrice joined in, "Who are
you anyway?" Before Matilda could

answer, Gemma scolded Beatrice, "Do
you mind? I'm talking to her. Who are you
anyway?" I glanced over at Dante

and saw him frantically punching buttons
on his cell phone. This redirected the
ladies' attention. Beatrice started

with, "Who are you calling and what did you
do with that cute little stocking cap I
knit you? You know, the one with ear flaps."

I didn't realize I had muttered
my 'Uh, oh' out loud. I could hear Dante's
muffled voice intoning, "Come on Virgil

"pick up," into his phone. Then turning on
me both Gemma and Beatrice said, "And
just who are you?" Matilda also stared

at me accusingly. Gemma rolled her
eyes and said, "Oh, brother. He's hitting on
mortal ones now." "Don't talk about

"my Dante that way," yelled Matilda. A
stern declaration from Beatrice, "He
was mine before he knew any of you!"

"Well," Gemma huffed, "while you two were swooning
over *your* Dante, I was changing the
diapers on *his* kids and washing *his* floors."

Beatrice wailed, "He didn't even wait
a respectable mourning period
before he married you!" Gemma pounced with

"I'm sorry you didn't live long enough
to clean up after him and put up with
all his dumb political cronies." When

Matilda crossed the river to defend
her chivalrous lover, the hair pulling
began. "Ladies!" I called out, pretending

I wasn't scared stiff. "Stop fighting! I have
a question for the three of you." They paused
in unison and glared at me. I gulped

and said, "Um, we all have to admit that
Dante isn't exactly Adonis.
What did you all see in him anyway?"

Unanimously they answered, "He is
from nobility," and they recommenced
their cat fight. "Ladies!" I began again.

"Instead of fighting over a very
old ghost, why don't we go shopping?" They stopped
as if quick frozen and stared at me. "Yes,"

I announced, "there's a sale going on in
the lowest part of Purgatory where
the world-weary souls are. Dante told me

"that somewhere down there is a cityscape
with a nice shopping area. " The three
female shades looked at each other and shrugged.

"I'm Sarah, by the way. Pleased to meet you."
None of them seemed to notice me as they
chattered to each other about dresses.

Dante was gone somewhere. Anandiel
guided me toward the next stairway.
The angel said, "Good job managing wrath!"

"Where did Dante go to? Will he be back?"

Canto XIII

nightfall, cornice of the lustful

"Dante got a call from Virgil," he said.
"Monday nights are when they normally play
Gin Rummy with Ovid and Cicero.

"Is it all right with you if I escort
you up to the next cornice?" Suddenly
I felt an inexplicable sadness.

Anandiel and I made it to the
top of the stairs and he found a place to
camp. Even if I wasn't exhausted

from the day's adventures, Purgatory's
rules prohibit climbing after dark. The
campfire that Anandiel built was

soothing and warm. He said, "It seems like we
should be making S'mores." I laughed for the
first time in quite awhile. The angel

casually added a log to the
fire, then said, "It sounds like you and your
Mentor have hit it off quite well." I blushed

and was grateful that the darkness could hide
my embarrassment. "Is something wrong?" he
asked. "Um, no. Of course not. I am tired

"though." With a gentle tease in his voice he
said, "Now, come on. Isn't that 'I'm tired' line
the one your family always uses

"when they don't want to talk? And doesn't your
family always back off, even when
there's something important to say?" Nodding

I buried my face in my hands, slowly
rubbing off the vulnerability.
Anandiel just stared intently at

me. It was obvious that he was not
going to let me rest until I shared
my inner turmoil. "Um," I began

stupidly. "Dante has been really great,
you know?" The angel just nodded. "I mean,
he's taught me so much. He actually

"saved my life a few times. Then again, I
shouldn't be marooned here in the first place…"
Still staring steadily at me. Silent,

demanding to hear more. I mean, I had
to keep talking, you know? "I'm embarrassed."
"About what?" I laughed and said, "You know that

"you sound just like my last shrink?" "You managed
to escape from her, too, didn't you?" The
angel leaned forward and resumed, "You were

"able to tell her about your parents'
divorce, your failed relationships and your
job burnout. You even allowed yourself

"to cry a few times. But you never were
able to tell her how badly you want
to die." His words were a sword, piercing me

to my very core. He continued, "The
disillusionment of knowing you will
never achieve your dreams, the disgrace

"of losing that job, the crushing blow when
your patient died, the emptiness and the
loneliness. And now the betrayal of

"your own body — just chronic pain joined by
the insult of getting old." By this time
my jaw had dropped and I stared at him in

disbelief. "How did you learn all of that
about me? I don't remember telling
anyone these things." The angel sat back

and said gently, "It's all in your Book of
Life. All the pain and your brave attempts to
disguise it. It's also in the hearts of

"those who so helplessly care about you.
It also recorded your compassion.
Now tell me, Sarah, what have I left out?"

"You probably already know," I griped.
"Yes I do, and so does Dante, but you
need to let the words out of your heart and

"tell them to me." Still hesitant, I said,
"You cannot tell anyone." With a slight
chuckle he said, "Angels invented the

"concept of confidentiality."
Under the stars with the soft glow of the
fire, everything felt so safe. After

a few moments I said, "I'm falling in
love with Dante and I feel so stupid
because he's dead and — I don't know what to

"think. There were times when he touched me and it
felt so nice. Then there were other times when
I reached out to him and he vaporized

"so that my arms just hugged nothingness." "Kind
of like the other men in your life, right?"
Again, the discerning words sliced through me.

"Anandiel?" "Yes?" "What if I also
fall in love with you?" "Don't worry,
angels can handle it." I thought about

it for a moment then said, "Angels have
a way of protecting themselves from that
kind of embarrassment, huh? An aging

"woman who doesn't get touched anymore
having sex fantasies about a ghost
and a crazy angel." I could feel an

angst rise again. Anandiel scolded
me now with, "Don't try to chase away a
painful love with anger." Then he wrapped me

in his arms and wings and held me tightly
with a very human embrace until
my tears fell on the gentle fold of his

wings. Still holding me, he whispered, "Eros
isn't the only intense love that two
people can have. Philia — the love of

"brethren for each other — can feel like a
kind of perversion and tragically can
drive those people apart. Agape — the

"divine love — can become so intense that
it feels like insanity. Do you know
why Dante chose to play cards with his friends?"

Still clasped in Anandiel's loving arms
I said that I didn't know. "He feels the
same way about you, and he told me he

"needs to talk it over with friends. You may
have noticed that he has had confusing
relationships with women in his life."

I chuckled, then said, "Yeah, those poets draw
women like a magnet, don't they?" "When he's
ready," the angel said, "he will return."

"And what if I'm not ready?" "You will be,"
was his response. "This cornice is the place
of the lustful, where sexual love is

"respected and courageously controlled."

Canto XIV

more on the structure of Purgatory

When the lovely sunshine awakened me
I was still cradled in Anandiel's
arms and wings. I quickly hugged his neck, then

backed away. Sheepishly I offered an
apology, "You really didn't need
to — by my estimate it's been about

"two or three days since I showered, changed clothes
and brushed my teeth." I tried to make myself
as small as possible in order to

contain my aromatic shame, but he
just laughed and brushed his wing against me. In
an instant I felt clean, refreshed and I

could detect a faint scent of lavender.
"Wow. Thank you Anandiel. I even
feel cleaner that when I woke up here in

"Purgatory." He feigned an offended
glare and stated, "I thought I did a good
job washing Hell off of you. The River

"Styx was pretty dirty for awhile
afterward." "You?" I exclaimed. "I mean you're
a guy — uh oh." Anandiel then changed

his appearance so that his hair flowed long
and silky and his face softened into
that of a woman. "Is that better?" he

asked. "Oh, Anandiel! You're perfect just
the way you are!" "And so are you," he said.
"Now we have places to visit and work

"to do." I asked, "Did you say this is the
cornice of the Lustful?" "Yes." "Isn't that
out of order?" He answered, "During the

"renovation of Purgatory they
rearranged a few things. You are really
going to love the new science labs. They're

"not like the ones you are used to seeing."
My memory flashed back to bottles of
reagents, electronics and a smell

of some unknown aldehydes (which, of course,
I was supposed to identify). "Um,
Anandiel?" "Yes?" "I don't want to sound

"arrogant, but some people have a hard
time with math and science." We ambled to
our next location while he said, "Do you

"remember that cocktail the pilgrims were
drinking back on the first cornice? The one
that Dante said was too toxic for you

"as a mortal?" "Yes," I said, wondering
how the angel, who wasn't there, recalled
that conversation. "For those who wish to

"advance to the higher realms, the tonic
increases one's learning ability
so that the learning adventurer can

"understand concepts which haven't even
been discovered yet on Earth." We passed more
small groups of students awaiting a new

lecture in a pleasant shady grove. "I
wish I'd had that in college," I muttered.
"The alcohol and drugs I used to

"experiment with didn't work too well."
"We all know that," Anandiel replied.
"It's one of the reasons you're here." I glanced

at him warily. "We *all*?" He halted.
"Not just I, but also your ancestors,
your living friends and family, and of

"course the keepers of your Book of Life." I
stood next to him, speechless. "By the way, in
case you haven't guessed, I'm your guardian

"angel." I smiled and impulsively hugged him.
Just as impulsively I blurted out,
"I love you! Um, is that OK to say?"

"Of course," he laughed, then plopped an arm around
my shoulder and tickled the back of my
neck with his wing. "Anandiel? Back there —

"is that how you knew about the tonic?"
He nodded. "I'm always with you, even
when you can't see me." I, frowning, "Then why

"did you let me mess up so much?" "Because
you didn't ask me for directions first,
and when you did, you didn't listen for

"my answer." I didn't like that. "Prayer
has a meditation component which
is where you hear that small voice, or see that

"visual image which can give you a
direction. And formal religion is
another vehicle for receiving

"guidance and support from other human
beings. Part of my job as guardian
is to stay out of the way of your free

"will while attempting to introduce
you to people, books, media and even
animals who can offer guidance." He

paused and stared at me expectantly. "I'm
waiting for you to ask," he said. I guessed,
"About the Book of Life?" "Bingo! You are

"indeed becoming more perceptive!" We
took our places among other souls. "When
the Divine Creator broke off tiny

"chunks of Itself so that those souls could live,
learn, grow and eventually return
to It, the Creator realized that

"It needed to keep track of those souls, just
as one would track serial numbers on
a valuable shipment. So, we angels

"were also created, but in a more
stable, non-evolving format, so that
we could each be assigned to a pilgrim,

"record his or her progress through life, and
be available whenever our charge
asked for assistance. You and I are like

"a proton and an electron." "So that
probably means we can't exist without
the other?" Anandiel smiled. "I think

"that's correct." "What do you mean — you *think*?" He
answered, "Even angels aren't privy to
all of God's will. What I do know is that

"the consciousness is too powerful to
wander through the multiverse without a
guiding spirit." I pondered his words for

awhile. "That really sounds nice," I said,
"but what if we get sick of each other?"
For the first time I saw a sad look on

his face. "A guardian angel without
a charge is a loose cannon. In Hell when
a soul has to be destroyed, they try to

"destroy its angel, too. Otherwise it
bumps around looking for another soul.
You know, weather anomalies and such.

"Lots of souls are being destroyed lately."

Canto XV

lecture on love, making amends

The angelic lecturer began, "There
are several types of love. Most of you
are acquainted with Eros – sexual

"love." A voice from the audience hollered,
"What will this lab session be like?" There was
a soft chuckle among the students. Then

a lightning bolt snatched their attention and
the instructor thundered, "If there's any
more disrespect you will be sent back to

"Hell!" There was immediate silence and
attentiveness. With great enormity
the teaching angel resumed, "Love is the

"most powerful force in this universe.
It contains the conscious force and the
creativity force. Curiously

"the love force also contains the forces
of entropy, in that love requires
balance in all things. The Hindus explained

"this in their worship of Vishnu, Shiva
and Krishna. The Destroyer is part of
this trinity beside the Creator

"and the Sustainer. Would anyone like
to postulate a rationale for this?"
The pilgrim souls' silent attentiveness

remained politely unbroken. "Could it
be that destroying old or redundant
or damaged parts of Creation are just

"as important as sustaining each new
creation as it appears?" The pilgrims
all nodded in agreement. "Could it be

"that you were all so terrorized by that
lightning bolt that you can't really focus
on anything I've said since then?" A low

chuckle from some souls in attendance seemed
to affirm the angel's speculation.
"I do have to apologize for the

"way I got your attention, but lessons
learned here are vital to your eternal
development. For those of you who choose

"to continue on to Paradise, it
is prerequisite that your spirits
are pure. You began by cleansing yourselves

"of ego constraints when you went through the
Pride cornice, then you learned a few techniques
for neutralizing Wrath by taking a

"fearless and searching inventory of
yourselves and admitted to God and to
another soul the exact nature of

"your vulnerabilities. Hopefully
you asked God to remove those defects of
character. Now on this cornice of the

"Lustful, you will learn how this powerful
force of love can be abused, or used for
your own spiritual development and the

"betterment of others. Unlike many
other emotional attachments, love
has many different manifestations

"including lust, loneliness whenever
someone feels unloved, the domineering
control of a beloved when the soul

"cannot or will not take an honest look
at his or her own needs, and love also
can lead to wars when patriotic love

"runs amok. Love can lead to jealousy
and violence. So many nasty things
can derive from such a commonly felt

"desire. Do you agree?" The students
sat obediently, nodding as the
angel smiled at them. "I see that you're

"still afraid of lightning bolts. What I showed
you then was my deep love for all of you
by way of discipline. Loving parents

"will not allow their children to play in
dangerous locations, no matter how
much the child cries and whines about how

"much he wants to play there with his friends. It
is a hard type of love to accept and
it's even harder to administer.

"Eventually you will all come to
love yourselves and others enough so that
you eagerly apply self-discipline

"in all your affairs. And, eventually,
as love fills your hearts and replaces the
old wounds, you will want to make amends to

"anyone you've harmed and forgive those who
have harmed you. This may seem difficult, but
many have gone this way before you and

"have felt the peace that comes from replacing
pain with love. Even Attila the Hun
came up to this level when, while in Hell,

"he became genuinely remorseful
for all the raping and pillaging he
did while on Earth. He has invested

"much work into searching for his victims
and begging forgiveness. Genghis Khan has
also come to repentance and truly

"struggles to pay child support to all
those millions of descendants he left
behind during his raids. There are many

"ways to make amends when we learn to love
unconditionally. In the same way
love takes many forms. We began to talk

"about Eros, or sexual love. There
is also Philio, or brotherly
love, Storge – the love of parents and their

"children, Caritas – altruism for
our fellow beings and Agape which
is love between God and His Creation.

"All of these can be characterized by
two different areas of the brain. The
primitive limbic system, for the most

"part, houses sexual urges while
the cortex expresses the higher forms
of love. Religions have, in the past, tried

"too hard to demonize sexual love.
It is essential to perpetuate
each species. Religious authorities

"have also perverted other forms of
love by promoting asceticism,
or a religious zeal which lead to wars

"of conquest over peace loving neighbors,
or a cloistering of people who should
have been out in the world practicing what

"they'd learned about love." The angel stopped to
look around the class. Some were too scared to
fall asleep while others frantically took

notes as if forestalling Judgement Day. "That
is enough lecture for now," he said at
last. "Your lab will consist of drawing up

"a list of people you've harmed and also
a list of people who have harmed you. Then
the discussions with other pilgrims and

"with your angels will revolve around how
to fulfill your need to forgive and to
ask forgiveness. Any questions?" No one

had any questions. Quietly every
student left to attend a lab. Dante,
once again wearing his robe and cap, said,

"They should have him teach the Pride section
instead." "Dante!" I exclaimed, then checked my
eagerness. He gave me a quick wink.

"Jezriel can humble 'em down so well."

Canto XVI

Dante and Sarah discuss their relationship

My mind and heart raced. Dante had returned!
Anandiel eyed me carefully and
said, "I have to teach a class. Do you mind

"if I leave you two for awhile?" "No
problem here," responded Dante. I, too,
said, "It's OK," although I doubted my

own resolve. Dante then nodded almost
secretively to Anandiel and
watched him leave. Turning to me he asked, "Is

"there anything you want to ask or talk
about?" "Not really." "Let's talk anyway."
I felt that leaden heaviness in my

gut that I've always felt whenever I
was in trouble. "You're wearing your robe and
cap again," I said optimistically.

"But what is the laurel wreath for?" He found
a spot to sit and motioned me to join
him. "Do you recall that saying, 'resting

"on one's laurels'?" I nodded. "Well, the wreath
is a sign of scholastic achievement.
It's like the colored stoles you see on the

"graduation robes of students who earned
Doctorate degrees." It didn't really
strike home until then just whom I had been

talking to. Stupidly I whispered, "You
are Dante Alighieri, the most
accomplished poet of the medieval

"world. You were a revolutionary
who helped begin the Renaissance." "I was
a soldier," he added, "a magistrate

"and a homeless, broke exile who would have
been burned alive if I had attempted
to return to Florence and reclaim my

"former social status. Yes, I am that
Dante. Last night my friends reminded
me of that, and of how ridiculous

"I looked in your twenty-first century
clothing. Therefore, you see me wearing my
traditional robes again. Quoting each

"other my friends told me to be true to
myself and stop trying to impress you."
(This man-ghost never ceased catching me off-

guard.) "*You* were trying to impress *me*?" I
gasped. "I may be dead, but I'm still a man."
Then he changed the subject. "Purgatory

"is where we come to grips with ourselves and
with our feelings, strengths, weaknesses, desires
and anything else that can keep us from

"Paradise." The grassy, tree-lined forum
was emptied of students now, leaving us
under a clear blue sky to work on our

feelings. I was too embarrassed to speak
so Dante said, "They should actually
call this the Cornice of the Love-Confused."

I smiled, my face still hot with a blush.
He resumed, serene. "This is one of the
more difficult levels to complete. Love

"is such a complicated emotion
because everyone feels it at some time,
everyone needs it and it's so piercing.

"A baby's very life depends on love,
yet as it grows the child resents the
helplessness it feels as it reaches for

"its mother for sustenance. Later in
life we cannot seem to free ourselves of
the continued need for love's strenuous

"intensity. It's strenuous because
so much work is required to maintain
relationships, and to understand our

"own feelings." Dante paused to admire
the pleasant blue sky. "You have seen my own
unfortunate relationships which have

"remained unresolved for hundreds of years
now. This is why I will not be able
to accompany you into Heaven."

Again shocked, I sat rigid and began
to speak. "But in your writing Beatrice
guided you through Paradise! You were there!"

With a negative gesture, "It wasn't
Beatrice. My own angel took her form
in order to appear less threatening.

"I realized after the *Comedy*
was written that my angel had arranged
for my visitor's pass because Lady

"Beatrice was no more able to lead
me through Heaven than I am able to
lead you." Suddenly frightened I argued,

"But you can't just leave me alone here! I
don't know how to get back.." "Relax," he said.
"You haven't met your guide yet. Don't forget

"that Anandiel is always there." "He's
always so invisible," I complained.
Dante responded, "That's what angels do,

"᾿ you know? Anyway, when I was with the
guys yesterday we were comparing notes
and they, too, said that parting company

"with their assigned pilgrims is heartbreaking.
All of us who choose to guide others have
to deal with the same pain of saying goodbye

"that we dealt with on Earth." "Then why do you
do it?" He smiled at me. "So that we learn
to stop fearing love." I contemplated

his words and felt reassured. "So what's next
on the agenda?" He stood up, offered
me a hand and said, "You and I will now

"wander to the cornice of Avarice
and Gluttony. I promise that these are
easier problems to deal with." We both

laughed and strolled toward the next stairway.

Canto XVII

the cornice of Avarice and Greed

"When Purgatory was reorganized,"
Dante explained, "it was decided that
the Avarice and Greed sections

"should be merged, as they are in Hell. It's now
a sort of a 'Materiel' Cornice because
hoarding, wasting, gorging and pickiness

"are basically the inability
to apportion God's material gifts
properly. Have a seat and I'll let the

"lecturer explain." The class area
looked the same as all the previous ones
with student-pilgrims casually spaced

around a pleasant tree-lined meadow. The
late afternoon sky promised another
rich, red-gold sunset with amethyst clouds.

The lecturer, however, was dressed in
rustic khakis and had a knapsack on
the ground beside him. I wondered how he

got the straps across his wings, or did he
carry it in front of himself like a
baby carrier, or did …? "By now," the

angel began, "you have all acquired
enough humility to realize
how much you need to learn, and you received

"a potion to help you learn it. You have
seen the uselessness of envy and wrath.
And obviously you have survived the

"lessons in love." A low chuckle warmed the
assembly. "Don't worry, I only use
lightning bolts when some student starts to snore."

Another chuckle. "Seriously, you
may feel pious, loving, humble and guilt
free by now, but the purpose of this cornice

"is to see how well those lessons have been
integrated into your consciousness.
It's easy to be virtuous when one

"is surrounded by virtue, but the test
now is to see how well all of you can
renounce sin when surrounded once again

"by temptation. Advancement to higher
realms is for souls who have that discipline.
There isn't much of a lecture this time

"but the lab part will be quite a challenge.
In fact, it doesn't take place anywhere
near to the Mound of Purgatory. Rather

"you will be flown in small groups to islands
which are part of our new renovated
Purgatory Complex. In addition

"your astral bodies will be made denser
so that you will once again feel hunger
and thirst…" The angel held up his hand to

quiet the displeased group, "…and in case of
a classical injury, you will feel
pain once again." He held up his hand and

continued, "Remember, you chose to go
this route rather than reincarnate. You
are no longer Freshmen or Sophomores

"to use an analogy. The coursework
will become increasingly challenging
and the prerequisite is to accept

"greater responsibility for the
eternal disposition of your own
soul. No more excuses or weaknesses.

"You already know that we all — even
angels — originally came from the
God-Consciousness. It was an agreement

"to go out into Creation, learn, and
ultimately return to the God-Force
to become part of Its restoration.

"To return to the body of God we
must all become as perfect as God the
all-loving, all-knowing, omnipotent.

"More will be demanded from you as you
proceed on this pilgrimage until you
reach the firewall purification

"which enables you to enter Heaven.
And once there you will only receive your
divine powers as your commitment to

"perfection is confirmed. For now, you are
all going on a camping trip." There were
murmurs of uncertainty within the

group of students. The angel in khakis
resumed, "Other pilgrims have completed
this challenge successfully. And others

"have not. Depending on which sin those souls
succumbed to they, unfortunately, had
to return to a lower level of

"Purgatory to repeat the lessons
they obviously had not learned before.
This experience will be similar

"to life on Earth, except there will be no
natural disasters, no disease, no
death and all food will be provided to

"you in the form of daily manna, which
is a nutritionally complete
pleasant tasting calorie source. It's the

"same food God provided to the Children
of Israel during their forty year trek
in the desert. You'll also have plenty

"of clean water for drinking and washing.
Your groups will consist of fifty to one
hundred pilgrims. With your physical needs

"met, the only challenge you will face is
the challenges of your own inner selves.
This is a test of your ability

"to live communally and to remain
virtuous in an environment with
fewer physical sufferings than you

"all met while on Earth. Any questions?" The
pilgrims were silent for a moment, then
one of them asked, "What kinds of sins did

"the others commit?" The angel answered,
"Good question. Most of the sins consisted
of hoarding manna, aggravating each

"other to the point of violence and
there were interesting variations
of lustfulness, bullying and stealing."

"Sounds like a breeze," said one of the pilgrims.

Canto XVIII

visiting a campsite

Dante accompanied me to a launch
site where hundreds – maybe thousands of souls
waited to board a type of huge airbus

which I'd never seen before. The hundreds
which embarked on airborne vehicles were
replaced by hundreds more. Each launched airbus

was replaced by another airbus to
collect the hundreds of pilgrims who had
replaced the previous ones. Turning to

Dante I said, "Where did all these people
come from? The classrooms aren't that large." He said,
"Hell, Purgatory and Heaven are so

"much larger than you can imagine. They
contain the souls of billions..." He kept
talking, but my attention was drawn to

the voices of some angels standing in
back of us. "They're pushing them too fast."
"Ever since (unintelligible) the

"pressure has been on to (something) (something)
and they're just not ready." Then Dante's voice:
"Sarah? Are you listening?" "Um, yeah. I'm

"just kind of tired is all." Straining to
overhear the conversations again,
all I could make out were words like, "…battle…"

"…the seals…", "…tribulation…" "Sarah! Hurry
up! Our pilot is waiting!" I quickly
apologized and jogged to keep up with

him. Again Dante began to explain
where we were going, why, and what we would
see. I tried not to look at him because

it only made my infatuation
grow. But I wished, and disciplined myself,
and wished. Finally I glanced at his hooked

Medieval nose and his drawn, high cheekbones
and told myself to imagine what our
kids would look like. It worked. "This is a new

"Purgatory feature, actually.
Saints Augustine and Thomas Aquinas
designed it as a result of a sort

"of wager. Augustine believed that Man
is inherently bad and, left to his
own devices, would degenerate back

"into evil. Aquinas, of course, said
the opposite — that Man is innately
virtuous and it is circumstance that

"corrupts the soul." "Who's winning?" I asked. He
gave me a dirty look and answered, "We
haven't been keeping score," he snapped. "OK.

"There were a few pilgrims who failed the
basic requirements that you heard in
the lecture." I apologized, saying

"It was insensitive, the way I asked
about how souls got along in other
colonies." His shoulders were slumped as he

answered, "I'm sorry, too. Sometimes the vast
enormity of Hell, Purgatory
and Heaven overwhelm me and I get

"a bit edgy." Then suddenly there was
a huge shudder, like an earthquake. Dante
and I reached for each other. The event

was too terrifying to feel any
embarrassment. "What was that?!" I shouted.
He pulled away from me and responded

with an eerie statement, "Changes." "What kinds
of changes?" I demanded. "Just the kinds
of changes that occur every now and

"then," was his rejoinder. He flashed a grin, which
I could tell was contrived. "You know, kind of
like resetting a clock." I viewed him with

suspicion. "Dante, you've been honest with
me and I trust you." Again he forced a
smile. "Really," he said. "The reboots are

"a bit nerve-wracking, but it all works out
as it's supposed to." Then redirecting
his gaze he grabbed my hand and pulled me to

a helicopter that was revving up
its rotors. "Come on! He's getting ready
to leave!" We ran past pilgrims and angels

who were also trying to board. Dante
shrewdly nudged them aside saying, "Bless you
brother," and "Yours is next." Finally we

got into the chopper and the pilot
seemed desperate to lift off the ground and
go. "Is there a problem?" I asked. Dante

answered with a dismissive, "David here
is just in the habit of quick take-offs."
The pilot was intensely focused on

his helicopter, yet he was able
to add, "Yeah. It's a habit I got in
'Nam transporting wounded from battlefields."

Dante looked at a map and said, "David,
we'll need to visit Island Gamma. I'd
like to show Sarah what an empty one

"looks like." "Sorry, Dante," the pilot said.
"Gamma's full. It looks like we found the lost
colony of Roanoke." "Oh, man," my

Mentor exclaimed disgustedly. "Quantum
entanglement again?" Then the pilot:
"Looks that way." "I thought someone fixed that glitch."

The pilot responded, "Development
Team's working on it for the release of
Purgatory 3.0." So I asked

"What's the deal with Purgatory three point
oh?" David and Dante gave each other
a questioning glance. With hesitation

Dante said at last, "Rebuilding is what
makes Creation alive and vital. It's
like the repairs that constantly go on

"in the human body. Three point oh is
just a routine revitalizing of
Earthlings' afterlives." Before I could ask

any more questions, the chopper landed.
The environment on Island Gamma
was that pleasant green landscape I had learned

to expect from Purgatory. Where the
trees and flowers and pleasant scents used to
comfort me, there was now that tight feeling

in my gut which always signaled me
that something wasn't right. We exited the
chopper, Dante and I, into a crowd

of genuine Pilgrims who seemed to be
peaceful and amiable enough. But
not far away I could see and hear

a seraph who appeared to be in charge.
He asked, with angry quivering wings, "And
where were the guardian angels when these

"transgressions occurred?" Another angel,
apparently a subordinate, said,
"Sir, a few of them were granted leave to

"listen to a talk on motivation."
The seraph growled, "For themselves or for their
charges? Never mind — that's rhetorical.

"How was the coverage duty ensured?"
The subordinate shifted nervously.
"Well, Sir, Naraphon took three pilgrims and…"

"THREE!" the seraph blasted. "You all know that
no guardian angel may take on more
that two charges for a maximum of

"one Earth-rotation! Fill out a blue form
and have all of the guardians involved
report to me — ONE.AT.A.TIME." "Yes, Sir!"

The smell of flowers drifted past as the
seraph swished away in a thunderclap.
Dante tried to block my view of the scene.

"Excuse me," I snarled. "I have some questions."

Canto XIX

cornice of science and technology, Dante leaves

We had returned to Mount Purgatory
to a quieter area of the
same cornice. "What's going on here?" I

demanded. "It's complicated," Dante
returned, "and to tell the truth, I'm not too
sure myself." I used the same silent stare

technique that Anandiel and three of
my five shrinks used when they wanted me to
say more. It didn't work. Dante must

have been a skilled politician in his
day. Instead, I found myself jogging to
keep up with him as he marched toward the

next stairway. "Dante!" I shouted to the
back of his head, "it seems like the last time
angels got into disputes, someone named

"Lucifer ran off with half of them!" He
slowed his pace, looked back at me as if to
answer, then resumed his determined stride.

We reached the next stairway and, short of breath,
I tried again. "Come on, man! I'm more scared
now than I was when we were in Hell." He

stopped then and turned to me. "As I said, there
are some things I don't understand either.
For now, the best thing for both of us to

"do is our assignments. Your job is to
observe and learn. My job is to teach you
what I know, and I'm rapidly reaching

"the limits of my knowledge base." He stared
at me intently. "Seriously," he
added, "there's indeed more activity

"around here than I've seen in my seven
centuries' sojourn, but I'm not lying
when I tell you that I don't understand

"it either. All I can do is show you
our math and science labs. You didn't see
anything written about labs in my

"*Divine Comedy* because it was all
so much more advanced than our level of
technology at the time and I could

"not understand any of it. So the
Church fathers simply re-wrote those parts with
my nebulous descriptions." I asked him,

"Which parts?" "I don't remember off-the-cuff.
I think they changed it into one of the
conversations I supposedly had

"with someone." We stared each other down for
awhile, then I gave in. "OK. I
guess I'm being kind of hard on you. What's

"next?" We stood at the foot of the stairway.
"So are we OK?" he asked. "Yeah, sure," I
said. "You're not mad at me?" "Nope." "We can climb

"these steps then?" "Sure." We climbed without further
conversation. When we reached the top of
the stairs the scene was vastly different

from the previous cornices. I gazed,
awe stricken, at an enormous college
campus which stretched as far as I could see.

"Oh my God," I whispered impulsively.
"Awesome!" Dante smiled and admired
the campus, too. "This is where I spend most

"of my time now," he said. "I don't know if
you are aware of this, but I was a
member of the apothecary's guild

"back in Florence. It was one of the more
science-oriented guilds and even
with our limited expertise, I found

"the discoveries of alchemists to
be absolutely fascinating. Of
course, I never dabbled in alchemy

"myself..." I chuckled and said, "Don't worry.
I won't call the constable." He, too, laughed.
"Did you ever find the Philosopher's

"Stone?" "No," he smiled, "but they have something
similar in the neutron collider."
Like a couple of freshmen we strolled through

the various types of architecture,
from neoclassical colonnades to
modern minimalist glass and metal

buildings that practically dared students
to enter the future. Dante told me,
"I've been busy for centuries trying

"to keep up with technology. I've gone
from horses to horsepower and I've learned
how to design software that would have had

"me declared a witch at one time." Pointing
to a translucent structure which floated
above a green commons, he said, "There are

"technologies here that our Creator
knows about, but mankind hasn't figured
it out yet. Although when I look back on

"Earth, it seems like you living beings are
getting pretty close." Then I teased him with,
"Like, I didn't know that ghosts have cell phones."

Amused, he replied, "I've gotten used to
it, but the reception in Hell is still
pretty bad. Actually, the upper

"classmen don't even use devices to
communicate. And if they don't learn how
to do it here, they'll learn it in Heaven."

Strolling through the crowded mall was a slight,
elderly gentleman who appeared to
be Asian, with his elaborate

robe, sandals and a type of headgear that
I once saw in a history book. He
slowly, deliberately made his way

to where we were standing. Bowing deeply,
Dante said, "Master Sun, we are honored."
The gentleman bowed and replied, "Master

"Alighieri, the honor is mine."
Not knowing what else to do, I also
bowed. Bowing again to the old man, my

Mentor said, "Master Sun, this is Sarah.
She is the pilgrim I told you about."
We exchanged niceties, then Dante said,

"Master Sun will be guiding you from here."
"Dante, no! There's so much I'd like to ask..."
He gave me a sad, heartbroken smile.

"We'll see each other again someday. As
my dear friend Virgil said before he left,
'Lord of yourself, I crown and miter you.'"

Then he kissed my hand, turned and walked away.

Canto XX

Sun Wun Liu

My Teacher, Guide, Mentor and Confessor
vanished, leaving me utterly alone.
I cried out for him, but my voice echoed

seemingly forever in that awesome
place. I wept and bleated for him like a
lost lamb. I didn't notice the other

figure standing behind me, patiently
waiting for me to turn around and look.
When my lonely tears prevented me from

seeing any of the grandeur around
me, his gentle voice finally began
to speak. "Hello, Pilgrim and Wanderer.

"My name is Sun Wun Liu. Is there a
way I can help you?" Still weeping I said,
"My master Dante has left me without

"giving me a chance to tell him how much
his guidance has meant to me, and to say
good bye to him." "He already knows, but

"he has his own journey to complete. You
wouldn't want to keep him from that, would you?"
I shook my head and suddenly felt that

I was as helpless and alone as I
was when Dante first came to me. At last
I turned to look at the spirit who spoke.

"I'm sorry," I finally said. "I don't
mean to be rude. Did you say your name was
Sun Wun Liu?" The slightly built man with

a stereotyped white wispy goatee,
pigtail and a huge grin looked back at me
and answered, "Yes. I already know your

"name. You may call me Master Sun. I will
call you Pilgrim because of your chosen
pilgrimage." I started to protest the

presupposition that I had *chosen*
this awful trip, but he interrupted
me by saying, "Of course you chose it. Dante

"asked me to cover for him so he could
hurry off to his Quantum Computing
class," Master Sun added. I asked, "Do you

"mean I will see him again?" He nodded.
"In due time. All that we need and all that
we love will come to us in its own time."

"I hope," Master Sun said, "that you have been
able to see the purpose of this trip
you have chosen to travel." I listened

attentively as he reassured, "It's not
Hell, Purgatory and Heaven as an
external reality, but rather

"it's the saga of the soul on its path
to completion. It takes a lot of work
and will power and dedication to

"master any part of this difficult
voyage. As you've already seen, there are
multitudes of souls who simply will not

"do the work – like those who choose to remain
in Hell – or who cannot do the work – like
those defective spirits who went into

"the Lake of Fire. The majority
of souls, however, just need to take a
breather at various levels of their

"travels. Some do this by repeating their
Earthly experience, some choose to stay
wherever they are for awhile." I asked,

"But what's next? I've seen how the souls in Hell
are punished for messing up while on Earth,
and how souls in Purgatory perfect

"themselves by purging negative thinking,
exercising strengths and educating
themselves. But what's next?" Sun Wun Liu

waved his hand toward the Heavens. "If we
are to become co-creators we must
not only have technical expertise

"in creating universes and life
which has the drive toward survival and
reproduction and exploration, but

"we must perfect ourselves enough to be
able to teach those lives how to control
these powerful drives and channel them to

"constructive ends. A co-creator not
only creates, but also motivates,
nurtures, judges and punishes with love

"just as a dutiful, loving parent
does. The multiverse is a fractal which
repeats itself on ever increasing

"scales into infinity. It lives, it
reproduces, it builds and then it dies
leaving behind the products of its work

"from the subatomic level to the
macroscopic level of the planets
and universes and ultimately

"back to basic forces and particles
to begin again. The multiverses
inhale and exhale. Black holes eat matter

"and energy, then flip themselves inside
out like the stomach of a starfish who
is feeding in order to grow and live.

"Everything around you lives, even the
rocks which vibrate so slowly that eons
are needed before they can break down and

"become nutrients for incarnated
souls who, after their journeys have been won,
create. And Creation creates, resorbs

"and creates again." I gazed at the stars
in wonderment. Suddenly, everything
fell into place like a jigsaw puzzle.

"By the way, you must control your racist
thoughts," the man said. "What do you mean?" I asked.
He replied, "You are thinking that I'm just

"a Chinaman, like your third grade teacher."
Embarrassed, I said, "I would never say
anything like that!" Still patient, he said

"You did not speak the words, but your thoughts were
quite clear. You still haven't understood how
much power lies in human thought. It can

"create and destroy, and when vocalized —
when thought becomes word — cities are built and
cities are destroyed. Lives are created

"and lives are lost. At the level of the
Infinite — what you call Paradise — you
need to exercise this level of self

"control. The consciousness becomes a tool and
a weapon. At the lower planes there is
so much interference and chatter that

"thought loses its focus. Here it's vital
to control all thoughts and all words as you
would control a spirited horse." I stared

at Master Sun, dumbfounded, and stammered,
"But that's a tremendous burden! I don't
think I can control my thinking that well."

He said, "You have already come this far."

Canto XXI

the Great Library

Within that heavenly campus strolled groups
of debaters wearing togas, scholars
from different eras in the garb of their

day engaged in passionate discussions
and lab coated scientists comparing
notes about their various theories.

Sun Wun Liu asked me, "Would you like to
pay a visit to the Great Library
of Alexandria?" My eyes widened

and I could barely breathe out a faint, "Yes!"
He smiled and said, "It's over this way,"
and pointed to a distant Egyptian

styled building. "The library may have
been destroyed on Earth, but here no knowledge
is lost." As we ambled over to the

site I asked, "Master Sun? May I ask when
you lived and where you are from?" "Certainly."
he replied. "You see me now from my lifetime

"during the Ch'in Dynasty when the Great
Wall was built. I was honored to be an
assistant for Ch'in Shih Huang Ti himself.

"It was one of my favorite lifetimes
in that I played a small role in building
the Great Wall. It was rewarding to watch

"the feudalism of the Zhou empire
become organized into a peaceful
and progressive kingdom which became the

"model for future Chinese emperors."
We covered a surprising amount of
distance in a short time. I overheard

brief snippets of conversations about
politics, philosophy, art, music,
science (which I didn't understand), and

historical reminiscences which
never made it into my textbooks. The
atmosphere was intellectually

charged. Every now and then we passed groups of
musicians and singers practicing their
art, whether European Baroque, or

modern riffs on blues guitars, or Eastern
classical temple music. Every type
of music I could imagine and some

I'd never heard sweetened the atmosphere.
We approached a building with Egyptian
hieroglyphics and bright colored portraits

of Egyptian deities festooning
the outside. Inside were walls covered with
scrolls, papyri and clay tablets – all the

assembled knowledge from earliest times
until the burning of the library
by Roman armies. Master Sun stated

"Beyond these columns are the gardens,
the meeting rooms and the research centers."
"Research?" I asked. "Yes, the Great Library

"was a center of new learning as well
as a repository of ancient
writings. The history of mankind from

"our earliest encounters with callers
from other planets are on that wall." I
asked him, astonished, "So the stories are

"true about space aliens?" He replied,
"Earth has been visited many times. The
Bible even talks about Nephilim

"interbreeding with humans in ancient
times. Our human race began as primates
who evolved enough to develop the

"intelligence, curiosity and
dexterity to eat of the Tree of
Knowledge, described in Genesis. Then these

"beings, who evolved from the dust of the
Earth as other creatures had done
were chosen by the visitors who kick –

"started our evolution by adding
their own DNA to ours. In a sense
they created us in their own image.

"Also contained in the Great Library
are charts and invocations written in
the original angelic language

"which Doctor John Dee and Edward Kelly
rediscovered in the 1500's."
"Angelic language?" I asked. Master Sun

answered, "Yes, it's a very powerful
spoken language from early Creation
which can vibrate sounds compatible with

"subatomic particles and effect
changes on a molecular level."
"That sounds dangerous," I offered. "It is.

"It took special codes known only to a
few chosen individuals to gain
access to those scrolls. Doctor Dee wanted

"to use the language to reunify
the Christian church. It is believed by some
that Dee and Kelly may have played a role

"in unlocking humanity from the
grip of the Dark Ages, but of course
that's speculation. At any rate the

"knowledge was too powerful for them and
they both died impoverished. That is one
reason why the Church always discouraged

"meddling with occult knowledge." I snickered,
"That and the fact that the Church censored those
ideas it disagreed with." Master Sun

said, "Organized religion has abused
its power in some shameful ways over
the centuries. It has caused wars, pogroms

"persecution of innocent people,
greed, hypocrisy. However, it has
also offered hope to many people.

"The value of formal religion is
in its community. It's being with
other hypocrites and studying ways

"to correct our own hypocrisy. It's
seeing the same people week after week
and forming the kinds of friendships that can

"sustain us during difficult times. It's
studying our holy books together
and trying to live according to them."

Suddenly there was another earthquake.
After a few terrified moments I
regained my balance and my composure.

"Master Sun, I need to ask some questions."

Canto XXII

angelic dispute redux

Looking through a set of columns I could
detect the stairway which led to the next
cornice. I could also see a small group

of angels who were apparently in
the middle of some sort of argument.
The words and gestures turned into pushing

and shoving. Then one of the seraphim
dropped into the midst of the group with
thunder and lightning and students bolted

in panic. We were close enough to hear
shouting but not close enough to discern
what was being yelled. With a pleasant smile

Sun Wun Liu said, "And what would you like to
ask?" "Um," I began, then pointed to the
fray, "that." If he had been Dante I would

have been less inhibited and could have
screamed hysterically. The pleasant little
man, still smiling, told me, "You don't have to

"be afraid to talk to me. Although I
do approve of your self-control in this
situation. Self-control is a good

"thing." An angel feather drifted in a
slow oscillating arc, then silently
touched the ground in front of us. He then said

"We need to climb the stairway before dark
anyway, Let's go and ask why they are
quarrelling." Still hesitant I said, "Um

"Master Sun, I've learned over the years that
it's not a good idea to walk into
the middle of a fight." More lightning and

thunder announced the arrival of a
second seraph. Sun Wun Liu just walked
peacefully ahead while I trailed behind

at a safe distance. I hadn't noticed
that Anandiel rematerialized
again and was accompanying us.

By the time the three of us were at the
foot of the staircase, the contenders were
starting to disperse. Master Sun and my

guardian angel exchanged greetings, then
Master Sun asked one of the seraphim,
"What seems to be the nature of this fight?"

The angel bowed deeply and said, "Master
Sun." My new guide also bowed and replied,
"Orion." Then the seraph, who seemed to

be named Orion, said, "As you know we
are all a bit edgy because of the
Apocalypse." I cried out, "What?!" Master

Sun motioned me to be still. Orion
then said, "I'm sorry, I thought you knew. The
world has already ended. The sudden

"entrance of all those millions of souls
into Purgatory has their angels
competing for space. You'd think they would have

"learned to be patient and wait their turn by
now." Master Sun clucked his tongue and, shaking
his head responded, "Lack of faith. 'In my

"Father's house is many mansions.' is what
Jesus said." Still panicky I blurted
out, "What do you mean by Apocalypse?!"

This time Anandiel gently touched my
arm, bidding me to be quiet. "Do you
remember," began Master Sun, "in the

"library I told you a bit about
the angelic language?" I nodded. "Well,
it is a highly structured tongue which not

"only contains names and conjurations,
but it also accesses the onset
of the eighth day of Creation. We must

"hurry to these stairs before the sun sets."
Anandiel practically pushed me up
the steps. Once at the top, Sun Wun Liu

resumed, "Anandiel can locate a
good place to spend the night." With another
bow, my angel sped off somewhere. "At the

"turn of the twentieth century, there
was a popular spiritist movement
and a group called the Golden Dawn stumbled

"across Dee and Kelly's work. The members
took on the task of psychically visiting
each of the thirty-three watchtowers which

"are guarded by angels whose names are in
the Books of Enoch, written by John Dee.
Well, the last watchtower is guarded by

"a celestial spirit named Babylon
who, as you might guess, is the selfsame Whore
of Babylon named in Revelation.

"To make a long story short, this set off
World War I, then World War II, and a whole
cascade of events followed. There was a

"population boom because guardian
angels of the hundred-plus millions of
casualties of these wars were pressured to

"quickly process their charges by way of
reincarnation or Purgatory
to prevent backlogs. In addition the

"souls who were resting in Purgatory
were encouraged to either advance or
become reborn in order to make room.

"The large numbers of reincarnated
souls caused the population explosion
which in turn used up resources and caused

"global warming and its consequences.
Well, you've read Revelation and Daniel
and Isaiah. I don't have to explain.

"The people left on Earth are computer
simulations now and there is a sense
of urgency because the computer

"memory is slowly being erased."
Outraged, I cried out, "How can a loving
God do something like that?!" Master Sun said,

"I offer you this challenge. You still do
not understand the reasons behind your
supernatural tour. So I say,

"If you don't like it, create your own world."

Canto XXIII

another campfire discussion

Our warm campfire was deceitfully
peaceful and even calming, although this
time it brought back memories of hellfire.

I was told that this would be my last sleep
in Purgatory because Heaven has
no nighttime. I glumly thought to myself

all this and insomnia, too. "Cheer up,"
Master Sun chirped. "There's a reason why
everybody wants to go to Heaven."

"I can't think what that would be," I muttered.
Anandiel added another log
to the fire. "Sometimes," said Sun Wun Liu

"your cynicism is humorous. But
for now let's have a serious discourse
about Heaven. My hope for you is that

"you will eagerly anticipate the
Heavenly realms." Then he resumed, "You know
that people for millennia have cried

"out for mercy and have begged to know why
God permits evil. While in Hell, Dante
began to explain that Evil does not

"really exist, therefore it's not allowed
by God. This important seventh day of
Creation is the time when God has been

"standing back and allowing humans to
hone their skills as immature creators.
The result has been amazing progress

"in medicine, building, technology,
the arts and even in political
arenas. The negative results are a

"greater awareness of suffering plus
Man's inhumanity to Man. Every
time a mother loses a child we

"all cry with her when she begs to know why.
We all feel the agony of torture
victims. We all feel the hunger pain of

"a starving child. None of the other
animals on Earth feel this way because
only humans, so far, have been chosen

"to be co-creators. Now, I have told
you that all knowledge, including that of
the Great Library, is being stored here,

"am I correct?" I nodded. "Well, every
traumatic occurrence everywhere on
Earth also impacts the memory banks.

"These memories of horrors past which are
imprinted on the Mind of God," he said,
"are slowly disappearing one by one.

"For example, do you remember the
pain you felt from that fatal stabbing wound
you sustained during the first Punic war?"

I was taken aback. "I remember
reading about the Punic wars but I
certainly never fought in any war."

Anandiel was deferring to Sun
Wun Liu, who continued, "That's because
God has been removing these memories.

"During the seventh day of Creation,
the mistakes the co-creator infants
are making are being dissolved in Time.

"Knowledge gained and factual memories
are retained for the learning exercise,
but everything else is a hologram

"which is being erased from memory
banks, otherwise the trauma could affect
the new Creation which is happening

"right now. Consciousness, of course, is being
preserved because it is a primary
force of nature. But everything you've seen

"around you which you consider real is
non-existent except in the constructs
of your mind. Are you following what I

"am telling you?" I sat cross legged in
front of the toasty, crackling fire which
probably didn't exist and allowed

my thoughts, delusions and emotions to
swirl in that ocean of confusion which
ebbed and flowed within the tidal basin

that I thought was my brain. "I'm tired," I
started saying, then an insight slowly
formulated and became firm enough

to verbalize. "So this Apocalypse
isn't really the end of anything,
is it? It's been an ongoing process

"for millennia and..." I lost my train
of thought to exhaustion. "Keep going. You
are doing great, Pilgrim." "...and this present

"confusion is because the Creator
is calling in all of Its Creation
to transform it into the New Heaven

"and the New Earth that I read about in
the Bible!" Master Sun smiled and said,
"You've worked hard today. It's time now to rest."

I leaned against Anandiel and slept.

Canto XXIV

commencement

I awoke the next morning cradled in
Anandiel's wings, as I had the night
before. He was like a living feather

bed, so soft and comforting I didn't
want to get up and face the day. He urged
me awake and Master Sun greeted me

with that big grin of his. "Today we'll watch
the graduation ceremony and
the parade of all the pilgrims who have

successfully finished Purgatory.
This is always a joyous time when the
pilgrims decide if they want to advance

to Heaven or remain in the Earthly
paradise here is Purgatory. Those
who choose to remain can choose vocations

which are commensurate with their talents.
Some will work as guides, as Dante has, some
will teach…" I interrupted, "Do any

"of the pilgrims get to sit by a nice,
sunny stream and drink beer?" Sun Wun Liu
rolled his eyes and said, "Oh, really," and laughed.

"Actually," he resumed, "they get quite bored
after awhile and start asking for
something to do." "On Earth," I quipped, taking

advantage of the lighter mood, "it is
usually the wives who ask if their
recently retired husbands can find

"something to do. Something outside of the
kitchen." Both my angel and my Guide laughed.
Then Master Sun said, "The festivities

"are this way." He got up and motioned for
me to follow. Anandiel joined us,
bringing up the rear. I had the feeling

that he was providing me some sort of
safety net, although I had no idea
what I needed to be protected from.

Master Sun happily marched into a
throng of pilgrims and angels who all seemed
quite jovial. Some talked excitedly

about who they were hoping to see once
they got into Heaven. A few pilgrims
talked about enjoying a beer along

the sunny banks of the River Styx. I
ambled toward the beer drinkers but Sun
Wun Liu took my hand and led me back

toward the Heaven-bound. A large group of
pilgrims were singing and dancing to a
hand-clapping rendition of 'When the Roll

'is Called Up Yonder'. Another group of
pilgrims – probably Lutheran – held hands
and sang a more dignified, 'A Mighty

'Fortress is Our God'. Yet another group,
maybe Baptist, just looked disapproving
while waiting for the ceremonies to

start. Then an angel wearing doctoral
robes stepped up to a podium and said,
"Before we start, I would like a show of

"hands. Which of you believe that, according
to the inerrant Word of God, the Earth
was created in seven days, that it

"is eight thousand years old, that Mankind was
created and not evolved, and that the
dinosaurs roamed the Earth with Man – they just

"didn't make it onto Noah's Ark?" All
of the disapproving pilgrims plus a
multitude of others joyfully raised

their hands with a murmur of excitement.
The speaker then stated, "I'm terribly
sorry, but all of you will have to go

"downstairs back to the campus and repeat
your classes in Geology, Physics,
Evolutionary Biology

"Cell Biology, Thermodynamics,
Organic Chemistry, Population
Genetics, Statistics with an emphasis

"on evaluating scientific
literature and Embryology"
Satisfied smiles faded into frowns

as the huge group was shepherded back to
the stairway. The speaker stood patiently
and waited until the grumbling pilgrims

were gone, then resumed. "Before I go
any further, I would like to thank all
of you guardian angels for your hard

"work, dedication and devotion to
your charges." Anandiel stood a bit
taller and I took his hand while giving

him a loving and grateful smile. "I
would like to reward you all with a day
off..." The speaker was interrupted with

a deafening cheer from one-half of the
assembled multitude. Anandiel
exercised amazing restraint, choosing

instead to just flutter his wings lightly.
The speaker raised his hands, attempting to
quiet the raucous angels, but instead

he had to wait awhile longer as
thousands of guardian angels sang a
couple choruses of 'In Heaven There

'Is No Beer'. Finally the crowd settled
down and the speaker could continue. "...but
as you know, days off are not part of our

"official policy. You'll have to be
satisfied for now with the knowledge that
you and your pilgrim can once again be

"a unified whole as soon as your charge
is qualified to reunite with the
Divine Creator." The silence allowed

him to continue uninterrupted.

Canto XXV

the Heavenly Pageant

Once the crowd had settled down, the speaker
carried on with his commencement address,
"The future of Eternity is bright,"

he said. "As I look out over this new
group of Purgatory graduates, I
have nothing but praise for all your hard work,

"faith and dedication to reunion
with our Divine Creator. You angels
will once again know the power of free

"will and you graduates will regain the
angelic powers you once had when you
unify with your guardian angels

"and become one entity again. You
will know the thrill of meeting entities
whose incarnations preceded yours and

"your collective consciousness can connect
with the greatest minds of all Creation.
Most of all, your experiences and

"ideas will meld with every other soul
and you will contribute to creating
a new universe. I know I don't need

"to remind you of the tremendous new
responsibilities you will have. When
you create, remember your previous

"incarnations – both the good and the bad.
These memories will guide you when you choose
your new laws of nature, math and science

"which will direct the evolution and
development of your new Creation.
Here you have learned the importance of self

"awareness, self-control and working in
loving togetherness with others. Your
journey to perfection will continue

"even after you complete your final
purification through the firewall."
I turned to Master Sun and whispered, "What

"does he mean by 'firewall'?" He whispered
back, "We'll talk about it later." "Dante
wrote about a wall of fire…" I said

as quietly as I could. Master Sun:
"S-h-h-h." Me: "But it sounds like…" "S-S-H-H-H!" So I turned
my attention back to the speaker who

had directed his speech to alumni
fundraisers. I noticed that several
pilgrims and angels were glancing at the

sun's position in the sky because they
didn't have wristwatches. The speaker told
the group about the way each entity

was split into two parts at the onset
of its journey through reincarnation.
The guardian angel half had direct

communication with the Heavenly
beings and retained most of its divine
powers, but it could not make decisions.

Decision-making and free will was the
prerogative of the pilgrim which lacked
divine powers but retained sensory

input. In this way both the guardian
angel and its charge reincarnated
together and purified together.

More pilgrims and their angels were gauging
time by the sun, so the speaker declared,
"Now for the event you were all waiting

"for. The Heavenly Pageant!" And with a
mighty flourish of its wings, the angel
transformed the commencement environment

into a parade ground. The sound of a
marching band grew louder, accompanied
by a choir of angels hovering

nearby. The music they played was lovely,
but the only ones who could recognize
the piece were a few souls whose most recent

incarnation was in Babylon. A
troop of baton majorettes led the
band, dressed in very modest Middle East

gowns from around 2000 BCE.
Sparkly multicolored starbursts glittered
along the parade route. The first of the

equestrian units followed the band.
They were an acrobatic centaur act.
The man part of the centaur flipped fully

human gymnasts back and forth and up and
down and everywhere in between, dancing
around the other centaurs and prancing

proudly down the causeway with tails waving.
Next came a tribute to Earth. Each epoch
in the planet's geological past

was represented by a colorful,
brightly lit float which was labelled with the
name of that epoch. Life-sized animal

holograms walked, swam, slithered and crawled
around the float itself and around the
audience. The Jurassic float produced

delighted screams as huge dinosaurs roamed
amidst the crowd, looking like they might eat
them, or trample them or both. The Cambrian

Explosion really exploded into
another starburst of color and light.
The Ice Ages float turned the ambient

temperature down a few notches so that

even the non-material spirits
felt the chill. One float after another

dazed the crowd with representations of
tectonic plate movements, mass extinctions,
slimy little critters evolving and

turning into slimy big critters who
swam and crawled into the audience and
transformed into more advanced critters right

where they stood. More marching bands played music
from all over the world, more fireworks
and more holograms entertained them all.

And the parade was only half over!

Canto XXVI

heavenly pageant

Conspicuously missing from all the
Heavenly Pageant gala were close-order
drills, cute little girl scouts flipping around

fake wooden guns, flags of any kind and
any type of military displays.
This was a good thing because the source of

so many wars — religion — was featured
next. An ornately detailed chariot
drawn by sparkling white unicorns honored

Jesus, Mohammed and Moses. The three
divine leaders agreed ahead of time
to ride together because disciples

used them too many times as an excuse
to wage another war. Even with their
show of solidarity a couple

of zealots in the crowd had to be forced
apart by angels and escorted to
Hell. Their chariot proceeded along

the parade route without further ado.

Buddha, Confucius, Quetzalcoatl,
Vishnu, Shiva and Brahma rode their own

chariots since their followers were a
bit more civilized. More chariots with
gorgeous detailing exhibiting their

cultures of origin were pulled by proud

unicorns. The gods and goddesses of
ancient Babylon, Egypt, Greece and Rome

plus ancient tribal deities from all
over Europe, Africa, Asia and
the Americas made their appearance

amid cheers and very old hymns. A herd
of flying horses (wearing diapers, of
course) added a third dimension to the

festivities by performing dressage
on a majestic scale. Their aerial
acrobatics delighted the huge crowd

with their barrel-rolls, swooping figure eights,
prancing up and down invisible stairs,
3-D square dance to heavenly music

gavottes, polkas and upside down waltzes.
All of these displays continued to be
accented with the sparkling starbursts that

originated from thin air. The grand
finale was delivered by angel
choirs and griffons who swept in showers

of flower petals and butterflies while

the entire sky lit up in sunset
colors, neon colors and night sparkles

with twinkling stars dancing a celestial
ballet. Before they knew it the pilgrims
and angels were standing in front of the

firewall which marked the borderland of
Purgatory. The spectacle of floats
and events slowly faded away. The

same angelic speaker who had addressed
them before the parade stood before the
graduates and angels again. He

waited for everyone to settle down
then, backgrounded by the purifying
wall of fire, he began. "Heaven is

"a place that demands perfection. It is
the source of all creation, and if your
creations contain traces of moral

"or spiritual impurity, then
the suffering of all the entities
you've created will be great. You still have

"the chance to return to the paradise
which is in Purgatory. However,
those of you who yearn to return to the

"Creator must pass through this firewall.
It is like a disinfectant shower
which removes the last impurities you

"may still have. It will not harm you or your
guardian angels and, yes, both of you

must cross it together. Ultimately

"you will both be reunited into
that celestial entity which was first
divided in half and sent into the

"cycle of birth and rebirth. Your work is
greatly treasured because you are the ones
who will regenerate Creation now

"and into Eternity. Creation
always existed and when you return
you will immediately understand

"the purpose of your long and oftentimes
arduous journeys. The melding of your
souls will produce a bliss that you will once

"again remember and you will know that
you wanderers have come back home. Beyond
the firewall is the River Lethe

"which will take away all memories of
guilt, which you no longer need to drive you
toward righteousness. Then you will bathe in

"the River Euno , which will restore
memories of all your incarnations
and the wisdom you acquired from each."

The speaker left the podium then, for
it was decision time. Each graduate
and angel discussed between themselves the

important task at hand. Were they ready
for the dedicated and determined
effort they needed for awhile longer?

Anandiel and I held hands and prayed.

Canto XXVII

the firewall, the River Lethe, the River Euno

Many graduates and their guardian
angels chose to turn away, returning
to the gardens of rest and repose in

Purgatory. Anandiel and I
looked at the massive wall of flame, then we
looked at Sun Wun Liu, then we looked at

each other with the same terror in our
eyes. The flames had to be at least ten feet
high and, peering through the firewall as

best we could, it seemed to be about six
feet wide. Gazing along the length of it
I could see other pilgrims and angels

hesitating like we were. "So when do
I finally get to wake up?" I said
under my breath. Once again I wished that

Dante was there. Master Sun piped up,
"You know that Master Alighieri
successfully walked through the wall while

"he, too, was still a living human and
he was unharmed. He wrote about it in
detail." Sensing our hesitation he

added, "Here, let me help you." Then boldly
Sun Wun Liu strolled into and through the
flaming wall. Once on the other side he

turned to Anandiel and me saying,
"It will not harm either of you. Among
other things, this is a test of your faith."

Once again, my angel and I exchanged
glances, then we held hands and plunged forward.
Master Sun kept encouraging us from

the other side until the three of us
were safely reunited. I exclaimed,
"I didn't even feel that!" I turned to

Anandiel and asked how he was. He
smiled and gave me a thumbs up. That was
when I realized that he hadn't said

a word since Dante left. "Are you sure you're
OK?" I asked. Master Sun suddenly
disappeared somewhere. "I'm fine," my angel

laughed. I scanned the area, looking for
Sun Wun Liu. "Great. Now Master Sun is
missing." "No I'm not. I just had to get

"some equipment ready. I am proud of
you both. That was a great accomplishment!
Are you ready for the River Lethe

"or do you need to rest?" Anandiel
kissed my hand, just as Dante had done. I
cried out, "No! Anandiel! First Dante

"and now you?!" My blessed guardian said,
"I'm not leaving you and I never will.
Guardian angels are only supposed

"to be visible during times of great
duress, and our journey from here on in
will be astounding, but not dangerous."

"But I need you!" I wailed. He replied, "And
I need you also. That's why I'll always
be here beside you, just as I've always

"been and always will be. Sometimes I don't
understand the rules, either, but there must be
a reason for them." Master Sun motioned

with his hand and my angel disappeared,
leaving behind a single white feather.
"Go ahead and pick it up," Master Sun said

gently. "It's nice to have a tangible
reminder of those we love, whether it's
a photograph, or a lock of hair

"or something our beloved made for us.
It's a comfort when memory isn't
enough." Sadly, I picked up the feather.

"Let's go to the river," I said with as
much courage as I could muster. My new
Guide touched my shoulder and led me forward.

The sparkling river was as beautiful
as Dante described it. We strolled toward
it in silence. I felt a strange lightness

as if a great weight had been lifted from
me. "It's the fire of purification,"
my new Master volunteered. It was nice

in a way, not having to verbalize
everything for him. "Tell me what you are
feeling," he said. "It's not good for a

"human tongue to remain idle for too
long." I giggled and told him, "I thought you
inscrutable Asian scholars always

"taught your students to shut up and listen."
"Not in your case," he said. Then he went back
to being inscrutable. At the bank

of the River Lethe, he took my hand
and directed me into the waters.
I waded in, unsure of what to do

next. Then I looked ahead and saw Sun Wun
Liu standing on the far bank, waving
for me to come to him. The water was

too deep and the current too fast. The next
thing I knew, Master Sun was pulling me
to the shore – while standing on the water!

Wet from the River of Forgetfulness,
I fell to my knees and gasped, "Master Sun."
"There is no need for that. However, if

"you are ready, the River Euno
is just ahead." "Master Sun! I feel so
blessed! So free! I want to praise God and thank

"Him for everything in my life!" He smiled
and led me to the second river. We
repeated the same ritual, but now

when I emerged, I sang out about the
new miracle — I could remember all
of my past lives! Everything made sense now!

I can only steal the words of my Guide,
Dante Alighieri, to describe
my sensations, my thoughts and my feelings.

"I came back from those holiest waters new,
remade, reborn, like a sun-wakened tree
that spreads new foliage to the Spring dew

"in sweetest freshness, healed of Winter's scars..."

The Paradiso 2.0

Canto I

introduction

After my sublime experience, this
was actually kind of a letdown. We
had strolled toward another classroom.

Master Sun, reading my thoughts again, said,
"Yes, it can be quite disillusioning
when one comes down from what we term here a

"'Revival Tent High'. Once the dopamine
wears off the *work* of a spiritual
awakening must start if a pilgrim

"soul is to continue walking the path
without falling into atheism,
fundamentalism or bitterness."

We came up to another clearing in
a meadow which looked similar to
the other classroom clearings I had seen

in Purgatory, except that there were
only three students gathered in front of
a teacher. "Pilgrim, you are allowed to

"stay and listen, but you must not disturb
the class. If you have any questions, ask
me later" "Master Sun," I whispered, "the

"class is so small." He answered, "Jesus
said, '...for many are called but few chosen.'
Now listen quietly." He exchanged a

quickly waved greeting with the instructor,
then we sat at the back of the small group.
Writing on a blackboard of sorts which seemed

to be suspended midair, the teacher
said, "Congratulations on completing
your Purgatory lessons. My name is

"Metatron, but you may call me Enoch.
I already know your names from all of
your incarnations. Purification

"in Purgatory and the training you
received there are only the beginning.
Are any of you ready yet to help

"create and maintain a universe?" All
three students indicated that they were
not ready. "Do any of you feel that

"you are truly an angel yet?" This time
the students looked at each other, puzzled,
and murmured different answers to the

instructor. He acknowledged them with, "Why
don't we start by creating a list of
attributes an angel needs to have." He

turned to the writing board. "There are only
three of you, you do not need to raise your
hands." Both hands went down. One student offered

"Angels are able to heal people." "Good.
Anyone else?" "Angels can fly," said a
different student. "Yes," the instructor

said. "Just call out your ideas." "Prophesy."
"Destroy wickedness." "Rescue good people,
like Sodom and Gomorrah." The list formed

itself on the writing board as students
spoke. "Angels can make words write themselves." "Yeah,
like the writing on the wall." "They can cause

"plagues." "Angels pass messages along from
God back to Man." "They can read minds." "They can
appear and disappear at will." Then the

mentor glanced back at the board and said, "These
are all good ideas, and you will learn how
to do all of these and more. It will take

"a great deal of time, practice and patience.
When you have understood these tasks to our
satisfaction, you and your guardian

"angel will be allowed to reunite
for the second part of your training." At
this point Master Sun turned to me and said,

"That is enough of this classroom for now.
We shall return here later. In order
to show you the advanced class, I will have

"to encase us in a pod to protect
you from the higher vibrations of the
students' energies, and also to make

"their thoughts understandable to you." He
waved both of his arms in a circular
motion, drawing an invisible globe

around us. I guess we were inside a
psychic spaceship which probably looked like
an egg of some sort. "What you will see and

"hear will probably remind you of some
science fiction movie you've seen. This is
because science fiction storytellers

"throughout the ages weren't writing fiction.
Whether their dreams were sleeping or waking,
their visions were sent to them to inspire

"others to reach beyond realities
with which they were familiar, then grow.
The most famous writers and some who are

"unknown merely transcribed the visions which
were inserted into their own native
genius." I tried to feel around our

capsule to gauge its dimensions, but there
were none. "This capsule," Master Sun began,
"is here to protect you from harmful rays,

"extreme temperatures and injuries from
rapid changes in acceleration."
Before I was fully aware of it

we had passed planets and stars which were no
longer twinkling little spots in the night
sky. Like the Voyager probes I could see

surfaces of distant worlds and their suns.
My own Sun went on the explain, "You have
become accustomed to designs like those

"of Hell and Purgatory. Heaven, though,
is not organized like that. It is formed
entirely of everything you have seen

"in Hell and Purgatory plus all that
was, is and shall be in space-time. It is
the past and it is all of those futures

"which make up the present. Most of all, it
is a dream of possibilities. That
which has, colloquially, carried the

"name 'Heaven' is actually the Earthly
Paradise found in Purgatory. This
actual Heaven is more than most minds

"can understand. For it is the Primum
Mobile of Aristotelians,
the Perusa and Prakriti of the

"Hindus and the Kabbalah of the rabbis.
Heaven's infinite mysteries have been
revealed to those mystics, scientists and

"philosophers whose intellectual
equipment was sufficient to attempt
translating the experience into

"words. Therefore, you will not be perceiving
Heaven as you have been believing it
to be." A stream of flashes darted past our

capsule, then disappeared into space. "What
was that?!" I exclaimed. He told me, "Those are
highly evolved souls whose energy can

"now be measured as gamma rays. They are
probably travelling to some other
interesting galaxy. Sometimes they

"like to travel in groups." "Do you mean like a
gamma ray burst?" Adjusting unseen knobs
on the unseen walls of the pod he said,

"It is the responsibility of
the students to avoid such destructive
accidents like that. Here you can see a

"classroom of newly advanced angelic
students who have recently united
with their guardian angels." I could feel

Anandiel's hand on my shoulder. Sun
Wun Liu gave a disapproving glance
behind me and the feel of that friendly

hand went away. "Your time will come, but for
now you must obey the rules," Master Sun
said gently, but with authority. Then

Master Sun relaxed and produced a white
feather from within his robes. He gave it
to me with that gentle smile and said,

"You almost left this behind. He is still
with us, you know." Gratefully, I took the
feather and caressed it the way I used

to snuggle with my old teddy bear. I
found myself stubbornly choking away
my tears, but my leaking nose revealed me.

Sun Wun Liu said, "Have courage, my friend."

Canto II

the advanced class

I watched joyful reunions of the five
newly formed angels as they tested their
wings and hugged the other angels. I longed

to see and feel Anandiel again,
and I believe he felt the same.
"Their first class will take place on an Earth-like

"planet to see one of the many forms
which consciousness can take. It is one way
to understand their own consciousness force."

Then he asked, "Have you ever wanted
to be an astronaut?" "No." "That is too bad,
because the class is taking a field trip."

Hopeful, I figured we could wish them all
a bon voyage from where we were. Master
Sun said to prepare myself for a jolt.

I started to tremble violently.
"I understand your fear, but I think you
"and Anandiel will enjoy this trip."

Still trembling, I felt in my pocket for
Anandiel's feather and I listened with
my eyes humbly lowered. I thought I could

feel Anandiel's hand on my shoulder.
"As I said before we arrived, this place
is a twin of Earth except there was no

"extinction event like the one which killed
all of Earth's dinosaurs. So now I would
like you to think carefully about the

"way the Earth would appear now if the same
were true there." I was almost too scared to
remember clearly my old lessons in

Biology. "Um," I began, feeling
very stupid. "The reason creatures grew
so large is because there was a higher

"concentration of oxygen in the
atmosphere." "Very good. Go on." "Maybe,
since the dinosaurs were so large and so

"plentiful, they would have consumed a lot
of that oxygen until they reached a
new equilibrium with the plant life - down

"to our present levels." "Yes, continue."
"So maybe the dinosaurs would become
smaller, like alligators did." I hoped

that was accurate. Master Sun asked, "And
what about the birds and mammals?" "Um, the
birds were probably more intelligent

"than dinosaurs because their brains became
proportionately larger. The mammals,
too, were becoming intelligent. They

"had to be because they had to escape
from both birds and dinosaurs. And being
warm blooded made them faster with quicker

"reflexes. The same thing with bird species."
I glanced up to see how I was doing.
Master Sun nodded his encouragement.

"So," I reflected, "would intelligent
life have evolved...?" I had to pause to think
about that. "I seem to remember an

"article which said it would be unlikely
that dinosaurs would have evolved into
an intelligent species because there

"was no need to." Sun Wun Liu nodded.
I lowered my eyes again. "Even if
they became smaller, they would have remained

"apex predators, because birds also
became smaller and mammals already
were the size of small rodents." "And how do

"you think mammals would have evolved?" I
had to think again. I pictured furry
little critters hiding out in their dens

waiting for the bigger critters outside
to leave so they could forage for seeds and
meat scraps. "Verbalize your thoughts please," he said.

"Um," I felt very stupid. "I'm trying
to imagine an intelligent race
arising from the dinosaurs, birds,

"mammals or even aquatic creatures.
The problem is, an animal has to
have intelligence *and* be able to

"build things in order to evolve into
a civilization, and a creature
needs hands to build. Unless it's able to

"mentally command another species
to do the building for it." I hopefully
looked to my Guide for cues. He volunteered,

"The second species would need hands also.
It appears that neither birds nor reptiles
were likely to evolve hands. The birds' limbs

"were developing into wings and the
reptiles were either remaining four-
legged or else their forelimbs were shortened

"into vestigial limbs used only
during mating to stimulate their mates."
I tried not to blush. "Yes, spirit guides know

"about sex. Now continue with your train
of thought." I focused again on furry
little critters. "The mammals would have had

"a survival advantage, though, if they
learned to become communal. And maybe
they would have learned how to reinforce their

"dens with either wood or some sort of hard
clay or rocks." "Metal smelting
is also required for advancing

"technology," Master Sun offered.
I nodded pensively. "Somehow I can
only see prairie dogs or a meerkat

"mammal species inhabiting the Earth
along with standard birds and reptiles.
Unless another aquatic creature

"were to crawl out of the ocean and grow
legs, hands, an intelligent brain, vocal
apparatus for communication

"and evolve all of this quickly enough
to avoid being eaten." I shook my
head. "I'm sorry, Master Sun. I just can't

"picture civilizations arising
without that dinosaur mass extinction."
He smiled and said, "Let's see how you did."

The space pod became transparent again.

Canto III

an alternate Earth

The view that unfolded before us was
that of a lush green paradise with birds,
insects, lizards and small rodents dashing

in and out of their hiding spots. "You have
done well," Master Sun told me. "Would you like
to step outside and get some fresh air?" The

air was so much fresher and cleaner than
any I had breathed before. Bird songs and
chirping animal noises happily

filled the landscape. A couple of lizards
stopped, studied us for a moment and then
lumbered off to whatever business they

had headed toward. Likewise, several
birds flew up to us and landed on the
ground before us before flying away

again. Master Sun tasted the fresh clean
air and said, "This is indeed a lovely
planet." More animals, birds and even

insects interrupted their busy days
to come up to us, pause, and then scamper
away. This was starting to get eerie.

"Yes, Master Sun. It is lovely here. So
this planet is as old as our Earth and
it went through the same changes over the

"ages?" Several small rodents came up
to us and, this time, actually seemed
to dip their little heads before running

off. I noticed that Master Sun also
dipped his head toward them. "Oh my gosh," I
whispered, "they're all bowing to him!" A small

troupe of bees formed a single file and flew
around his head, forming a halo. Then
the long line flew into a nearby forest.

Instinct dropped me to my knee and I, too,
bowed before my Guide. "Pilgrim, there is no
need for that." He reached for my hand and made

me get up. "I brought you here," he resumed,
"to show you that even these creatures have
the consciousness force. And when they die or

"when they are eaten, that force leaves them to
transfer elsewhere." I asked, "Are they aware?
Do they think? What about being eaten?

"Don't they get scared? Where do they go when they
die?" I suddenly remembered who I
was talking to, muttered a quick, "...sorry..."

and fell silent again. I thought I heard
him chuckle a bit before he said, "It
is good to have questions. All life is a

"miracle and when one finally sees
the entire scope of that miracle
it is overwhelming. Eventually,

"however, you will learn to center your
energy and direct your thoughts in a
more disciplined manner." We strolled around

and enjoyed the warm sunny day. "Let me
try to answer your questions." We strolled past
trees which (I do believe) moved their branches

the slightest bit as Master Sun walked by.
"Yes, all creatures who have evolved up to
a certain level have awareness of

"themselves. And, as far as their sensory
organs allow, they are aware of their
surroundings. The most primitive creatures

"have minimal awareness. Their force of
consciousness is what makes them alive, but
it doesn't manifest much further than

"that. The consciousness is attracted to
newly forming life, whether in eggs or
in fetuses or in seed pods. This, then,

"is the basis of reincarnation.
As Hindus claim, an animal can gain
merit and be reborn a new species.

"Now organize your thoughts and ask me your
next question again." I took a deep
breath, tried to slow my racing mind, and thought

again about animals killing and
eating other animals. "I'm bothered,"
I said, "about having to eat plants and

"animals in order to live. Is there
some other way? A steak used to be just
a steak, but now I see a cow dying

"and being cut up so I can eat its
muscles. And I even kill living plants
by eating them. Is there some other way?"

I choked down the nausea, but I let
a tear form. Master Sun studied me for
a moment then said, "I approve of your

"empathy for the living creatures you
feed on. Not many people also feel
such respect for plant life. I encourage

"you to keep exploring these emotions.
No living creature cherishes the thought
of being killed and consumed. In fact, no

"creature which lives truly wants to die. The
importance of death is that it forces
us out of our familiar bodies

"so that we must face the uncertainty
of growth. A surprising percentage of
individuals would rather die than

"face uncertainty. So to consume the
physical remains of a creature that
once lived is not, therefore, immoral. The

"dilemma of killing one's food also
precludes judgement because death cannot be
avoided. The only killing which is

"evil is senseless killing, as in war,
murder and avoidable accidents.
The simplest animals have an instinct

"to survive, which compels them to avoid
danger. Plants, of course, cannot move away
from a threat, but they are blessed with no brain

"to remember the trauma of losing
their limbs. Otherwise, plants would give up and
die as soon as a rabbit chewed on them.

"Carbon is food — souls are eternal."
Master Sun studied my face, then said, "There
is something which is still troubling you."

I replied, "Only the mass extinction
of the dinosaurs allowed humans to
evolve. Otherwise life on Earth would be

"the same as life on this planet. A freak
accident is the only reason why
humans and our ancestors came to be."

He grinned. "It wasn't a freak accident."

Canto IV

back at the beginners' classroom

We settled the pod back where the lower
angel trainees were now getting lessons
in yoga. Master Sun said, "We will be

"skipping back and forth between different
levels of training because even with
a protective pod, it is not a good

"idea to keep an incarnate human
for too long in the extremes of deep space."
I tried to feel reassured by that. A

look around the familiar classroom
area revealed three angel trainees
sitting in lotus postures with their eyes

closed. "What are…" I began to whisper. "S-s-h-h."
I watched silently for a very long
time, then shifted my stance just enough to

make a twig on the ground audibly snap.
"S-s-h-h.!" Finally Enoch let the students
come out of the pose. A peaceful feeling

remained in the class as he said, "So far
I haven't taught you anything that you
wouldn't have already learned in a new

"beginner's yoga class. The key here is
daily practice with the fundamentals,
to instill patience and willingness to

"continue the training. Our exercise
today will be the first thing we will do
before every lesson. It may become

"boring or even frustrating, but I
promise you will eventually see
results. It is the discipline itself

"which teaches. By way of encouragement
let me show you a few of the skills you
can achieve by learning this discipline."

Suddenly, Enoch unfolded his wings
and rose above the meadow, then vanished,
then reappeared next to me and Master

Sun. They exchanged wry glances and Master
Sun told him, "Watch the ego, Metatron."
"It's only for the benefit of the

"students," laughed Enoch, then he reappeared
in front of the class and presented more
material on yoga history.

Astounded, I stood speechless for awhile
then asked, as humbly as I could, "Master
Sun, would you be able to teach me these

"powers?" He clasped his hands solemnly in
front of himself and closed his eyes, seeming
to be in a meditative state. Then

shaking his head with a certain sadness
he replied, "Are you sure you want to learn
any of these psychic powers? Along

"with them comes great responsibility.
For now I have blocked your undisciplined
thoughts so that you do not harm yourself or

"others, and so that you do not perturb
the order of this universe. If I
had not blocked you, then and old childhood foe

"named Eddie Warren would be dead by now."
"Who?" I exclaimed. "I — um — no, really? I
haven't even thought about him in years!"

Master Sun raised his hand to silence me.
"You only believe that you haven't done
so, but he is still there in your mind like

"a very old and faint scar. This is why
I have stressed for you the importance of
absolute self-control in the higher

"realms. Completing the purification
of Purgatory is prerequisite
to entrance into Paradise for this

"reason." "But what if...?" "Do not worry. None
can enter Paradise without cleansing
themselves first in Purgatory. The soul

"cannot generate enough energy
to cross the threshold." "But how did I get...?"
Again waving his hand, Sun Wun Liu

answered, "You are not actually in
Paradise right now. You are on a sort
of visitors' platform which is used to

"demonstrate the wonders of Paradise
without becoming directly involved
and without contaminating the realm.

"Your friend, Master Alighieri, was
also allowed only this much access
during his human visit. 'Beatrice'

"made sure that he was protected as you
are and that Heaven remained free of all
impurity, although he did not know

"this. His technology at the time was
not advanced enough to even raise these
questions in his *Comedy*. Soon you will

"see a small group of advanced students come
here to tutor the beginning students.
A vital part of learning is learning

"how to teach. Most Earthly disciplines know
this and require their advanced students
to take on classroom responsibilities

"as part of their own curricula. Here
they come now. Please show them the same respect
that you would show any of your elders."

Three impressive angels appeared just then.

Canto V

beginners and their tutors

The three upperclassmen angels settled
amid the new angels. Greetings and joy
were exchanged among the six spirits. I

watched them with Master Sun beside me, and
felt a longing to be part of that group.
"Verbalize your thoughts, please," he said to me.

As if awakened from a trance, I told
him, "Huh? Um, I don't know. I guess I'm just
astounded at everything that has gone

"on around me." He eyed me seriously.
"You need to become more truthful about
your feelings. That truthfulness requires

"as much courage as your recent space trip.
Please trust me enough to share what you are
really feeling right now." He waited. I

told him with hesitation, "I feel left
out. They're all so happy and I know I'm
supposed to be, too, because we are in

"Heaven." I felt embarrassed. Master Sun
put his hand on my shoulder and said, "This
is such an easy problem to handle.

"Let's just go up and say 'hello'. It is
the same thing you need to do when you are
on Earth." "But Master Sun, I'm confused. You've

"told me not to speak several times and
now you want me to go up to a group
of strange angels I've never met and say

"'hi!'." He then said, "You need to first of all
share your thoughts and feelings with me. This is
part of your discipline. Then you need to

"trust my instruction. Now let's be happy
and meet some new friends." We strolled up to the
angels, and, still not knowing the proper

way to greet an angel, I introduced
myself. My greetings were met with such warmth
and kindness that I could not remember

the last time I'd felt so happy. Master Sun
then said, "Now remember how lonely you
just felt when you see someone else standing

"alone and forgotten." "I will, Master
Sun." Just then Enoch, or Metatron, was
standing among us. "Sandalphon, old friend,"

he declared cheerfully. "I haven't met
your mortal friend yet." He clapped a hand on
my head and said, "An angel's blessing on

"you, Child." Master Sun grinned and told him,
"Sarah is a pilgrim who is here on
special dispensation, to learn about

"the life after life." Directing us to a
different group of students, Enoch said, "Well
then, let's meet a group of students who are

"further along in their studies." We strolled
over to a group of ten, maybe twelve
students – some of whom were levitating

while others focused on making a few
rocks disappear. "By the way, Sandalphon,
why so reticent? Tell Sarah who you

"really are." Master Sun gave a quick dip
of his head and then said, "In order to
keep from intimidating you more than

"I already have…" he told me with an
uncharacteristic wink, "I took on
the appearance of one of my past lives

"which I thoroughly enjoyed. I was Sun
Wun Liu during the Ch'in Dynasty.
I served in the emperor's court as an

"engineer where I helped to design the
Great Wall of China. It was exciting
to be part of such a grand project in

"such an enlightened time, when Mongol hordes
were kept away so that law and culture could
flourish. During my most recent incarnation

"I was known as Elijah the prophet."
I'm sure my mouth dropped in amazement. I
quickly tried to remember as much as

I could from the Hebrew Bible. "Weren't you
the one who didn't die, but were carried
up to Heaven in a fiery chariot?"

"Yes," he replied. "And so was Enoch here.
You do remember Enoch, correct? The
father of Methuselah?" The facts came

so fast my head was starting to spin. "Here,"
Master Sun motioned, "have a seat." There was
no seat. He motioned again and a large

overstuffed recliner appeared. Gladly
I settled into the luxurious
softness, which reminded me of my own

Anandiel. The two gentlemen joined
me. "Master Sun?" "Yes?" "May I ask you a
rather personal question?" "Yes." "Who are

"you now?" "I am Sandalphon, another
archangel. I chose to appear to you
as Wun Liu because it would be less

"stressful for you. Sometimes an archangel's
appearance can drive people insane." "Speak
for yourself, Sandalphon," laughed Metatron.

Master Sun, or Sandalphon, gave Enoch
a playful leer. "Back at you, my brother."
Without thinking I blurted, "Gabriel

"was kindhearted to the Virgin Mary
when he told her she was pregnant... Oops! I'm
sorry. I spoke out of turn." Master Sun

or Sandalphon, gave me a slow nod in
acknowledgement. "Gabriel can be quite
gentle whenever he is not wrestling

"with someone in the desert or blowing
his trumpet to announce the End of Days."
I suddenly had that lead ball feeling

I get in the pit of my stomach plus
trembling limbs I feel whenever I
am terrified. "You'll be all right," he said.

"Shall we continue with our lesson now?"

Canto VI

lessons on directing the Will

Enoch was the one who explained, as we
watched the upperclassmen angels work with
the beginners, "The more advanced students

"are teaching the newcomers how to use
their will to channel their consciousness
in various ways. Shall we listen in?"

The two great angels escorted me to
a place where I could hear a tutor tell
his student, "The free will is like a Higgs

"boson which can connect one or more of
the natural forces with consciousness
to effect a change in ordered mass. When

"you did your *samyama* exercise and
directed your concentration on that
lesser known chakra, your will connected

"with the gravitation force and allowed
your consciousness to transport you the way
it did. Another way to propel your

"consciousness to, let's say a different part
of the galaxy, is to locate your
twin double over there and by way of

"quantum entanglement simply transfer
your consciousness into your twin. You'll find
it's much faster than teleportation."

The tutor and the student grinned at each
other triumphantly. Suddenly, a
distant rumbling accompanied a slight

shudder of the ground we stood on. Enoch
glanced at Master Sun and, leaning into
him, asked softly, "How's Gabriel handling

"the workload?" "He is fine," replied my Guide
softly. "He has prepared for this for a
very long time." Alarmed, I tried

to overhear more, but the two angels
turned back to me, smiling again. Master
Sun started to point out another pair

of students who were learning how to turn
one substance into another, but then we
felt another slight shudder. "What's going

"on?" I demanded. Enoch gave me a
quick smile, then answered, "It's just the Earth
remodeling project again." "What do

"you mean by 'remodeling'?" I
questioned, ignoring the fact that I was
speaking to an archangel. "You know, the

"eighth day of creation. The new Heaven
and the new Earth. Purgatory has been
done over for quite awhile now, and

"of course, Hell is being finished right now."
I stared at Enoch, then at Master Sun
who looked away. "Forgive my boldness," I

verbalized, "but how many people just
died on Earth?" Master Sun didn't look at
me, he just replied, "About six thousand."

Quickly Enoch added, "Their guardian
angels are working hard to get them to
Purgatory, and there is plenty of

"room for everyone now with the rehab."
I just stood there for a moment, trying
to take it all in. Then Master Sun spoke.

"Perhaps you can understand now my sense
of urgency, perhaps my abruptness
at times. We are working under a time

"constraint to show you what you need to learn."
"But why me?" I asked. "Why not you?" Enoch
replied. "Somebody has to carry the

"message. It may as well be you." I felt
resentful and manipulated, but
mostly I had a sinking feeling that

I was witnessing an arbitrary,
unguided flow of the universe. And
another panic arose within me.

Interrupting my thoughts, Master Sun said
willfully, "Nothing is arbitrary
here. You are being given a gift which

"can bring comfort to many of your kind
during a difficult upheaval. It
was believed that you would accept the chance

"with some eagerness. I have come to know
you well enough to know that, despite your
weaknesses and your fatigue, that you care

"very deeply about those around you
and about your planet. Now, would you like
to continue your lessons?" Somehow, I

managed to give him my consent, but
I still wished desperately that I could
wake up or something. Turning again to

his more authoritative mien, Master
Sun said, "The cosmos is filled with wonders
which have only been hinted at in the

"minds of writers and film makers. If you
have rested up enough, I would like to
show you another of these wonderful

"realities." I glanced over toward
Enoch, who indicated that he had
to attend to his own students. He and

Master Sun exchanged departing regards
and I quickly voiced a 'thank you' to my
visiting Mentor. Lecturing again

Master Sun said to me, "On our last field
trip you voiced an admirable concern
about eating live plants and animals.

"Would you like to see a planet where there
is no killing and no violence for
the procurement of nourishment?" "Is

"there one that exists?" "Yes," he replied. "All
nourishment for all living creatures there
comes from their two suns. Unlike our carbon

"based evolution on Earth, there was no
need to evolve genetics which favors
the most aggressive organisms in

"a 'kill or be killed' environment." "Yes,"
I told him. "I am ready to see something
serene and peaceful." He smiled and said,

"I believe you will enjoy this planet."

Canto VII

the silicon planet

We entered the pod and shortly we touched
down onto a stark brown world with two suns,
not as bright as ours, illuminating

opposite ends of the sky which was a
brownish red. There were strangely shaped creatures
which lumbered about slowly while waving

tentacle-like arms. "I've brought you to a
planet where there is no violence or
aggressive winners nudging out other

"rivals. This capsule is protecting you
from intense heat and the nitrogen-rich
atmosphere. Those creatures you see moving

"around are sentient beings who have
built amazing cities which are out of
our sight. Their bodies are silica based

"rather than the much more common carbon
based life found elsewhere. I am showing you
this planet because of its uniqueness.

"These are animal-like creatures which get
their energy from photovoltaic
cells on their skin rather than from breaking

"down other carbon plants and animals
for chemical energy. Therefore there
is no need to pick plants or to hunt food

"animals. Violent tendencies did
not become part of their genetics since
they were not needed for their survival.

"Their bodies do not create waste which can
soil their environment, and they need
very few natural resources.

"Because the solar cells on their skin makes
electricity and their nerves are kind
of like silicon chips in computers,

"they are highly intelligent, they
can process information much quicker
than carbon based organisms, and they

"have learned to focus their consciousness the
way a laser beam focusses scattered
light into a very powerful ray.

"From this they have learned how to levitate —
a useful skill for slow moving creatures —
and they can dissemble, then reconstruct

"anything they have built." "Wow," I gasped. "How
do they do that?" "It is complicated,"
Master Sun said, "but basically they use

"their consciousness to counteract the force
of gravity. When consciousness directs
the strong nuclear force, materials

"can appear and disappear and move at
will." I shook my head in disbelief. Then
I said, "Powers like this sound dangerous."

"For humans they most certainly would be."

Canto VIII

more on the silica planet

Master Sun continued, "It is good that
you are thinking about things like this. In
the human species, these powerful tools

"would, in fact, be at risk of being used
capriciously. This civilization,
however, has been carefully observed

"for millennia and they show no signs
of irresponsibility like that."
I asked, "What could anyone do, though, if

"they did?" Sun Wun Liu looked severe. "Those
types of entities are almost always
detected in the lower realms and are

"destroyed." "But isn't the destruction of
one entity by another evil?
Who would destroy the evil entity?

"Wouldn't the act of destruction make the
virtuous, policing entity an
evil one? Where do we draw the line?" Sun

Wun Liu responded, "The rule of Law
controls not only the behavior
of living beings, it also controls

"the movements of planets and the orders
of equations." While we were talking,
a city had sprung up around us. "Wha...."

I stuttered, but I couldn't even think
fast enough to formulate a question.
Master Sun smiled. "Because of their quite

"advanced abilities, the beings of
this planet move their cities to where they
are needed at that moment. It conserves

"natural resources, materials,
and it doesn't leave behind abandoned
cities which collapse." Noting my puzzled

expression he added, "Remember, if
you will, what I said about dissembly
and reassembly of objects with the

"focused consciousness." He reached for what seemed
to be an invisible knob on an
invisible bulkhead. "Let me show you

"something else that I think you will like." He
turned the 'knob' and I could hear something like
music surrounding us. A series of notes,

not at all unpleasant, were played in a
seemingly random melody. They had
a delicate chiming quality which

I found myself enjoying. Smiling, he
told me, "They are speaking to each other."
"Through music?" I asked. "In a way," he said.

"Because they photosynthesize, they do
not eat. Therefore they evolved without a
GI tract. They do not need a mouth, so

"they are unable to form words as we
do. However, they do have a breathing
apparatus which processes the air

"of this planet much as our own does. Now,
since most of their nervous systems consist
of metals, their bodies have acquired

"vocal chords which also contain metal
strings. By adjusting the tension on those
strings and exhaling on them, they produce

"the sounds you hear. Each note represents a
word or phrase. You cannot hear the lowest
or highest notes they produce. It is nice

"for their musicians who can write music
and lyrics at the same time. Also they
express agreement as chords — major chords

"are full agreement, minor chords are an
agreement under protest. The seventh,
ninth and various diminished chords are

"ways of requesting a recall vote or
an ad hoc committee, or any of
those marvelous little democracy

"inventions that exist." I thought about
it for awhile, then said, "A hotly
contested argument would sound like an

"orchestra tuning up." "Above certain
frequencies and pitches," he answered, "an
ear-shattering blast sounds from within the

"planet's core. The mechanism of this will
take too long to explain. At any rate
the sound is so dissonant and painful

"that compromises are reached quickly." The
city began to disintegrate, then
reappeared on the horizon before

our very eyes. The tall buildings with their
antennas and the pedestrians soon
rebuilt themselves just as they were before.

Master Sun remarked, "Apparently they
decided we were harmless visitors."
"What would happen if they decided we

"were a threat?" He replied, "Typically they
move the intruder to a different
part of the galaxy, preferably

"the intruders' own star system. Although
there are other planets where potential
felons can be sequestered. It's all quite

"genteel." I asked, "Are there other planets
or civilizations like this one?" "Yes."
"Then why haven't we been able to get

"any contact with them?" He looked at me
askance and said, "Do you mean to say that
all of those UFO sightings were not

"enough evidence of their attempts to
communicate?" "Well, yeah, but nobody
really accepts it as definitive

"proof. Besides, we need to hear in their own
words who they are and what they want." "What they
want," he said, "is to remain untarnished

"by humans." "Huh?" "Human beings are slobs.
Humans have soiled their own nest with trash
and polluted their own water and food.

"Other civilizations have taken
millennia to purify themselves
and their planets." "And they don't want dirty

"tourists like us to visit them?" "Correct."
I was actually starting to enjoy
this space tourism. "Is there more to see?"

With a grin, Master Sun said, "But of course!"

Canto IX

a parallel universe

We were still in the pod. I was watching
lights whiz past us, reminding myself that
those lights were massive stars. More 'gamma rays'

appeared and disappeared from view. "Master
Sun?" " Yes?" "Dante kept saying that the souls
in Hell and Purgatory were really

"in other universes." "Also in
other dimensions," Master Sun added.
"Oh, yeah. I forgot about that." I felt

stupid again. "Do you have a question
for me?" Another star cluster rushed past.
"Are we in another universe now?"

"No, Pilgrim. We are travelling in the
same universe with the same dimensions
you have been accustomed to." I stated,

"Oh, good. With everything so mind blowing
it's nice to know I'm within a few light-
years of home, at least." "I understand," he

answered. "We have been asking a lot from
you, and you have done very well. But now
I would like to take you into a new

"learning zone again." I felt around for
Anandiel's feather, then said, "Where to?"
He began another lecture. "Have you

"noticed how many pairs of opposites
occur in Nature?" I nodded and said,
"Male and female, positive / negative

"electrodes, acids and bases, pairs of
quarks." "Exactly," he said as I felt the
pod come to a rest. I couldn't see any

movement outside. Only darkness. He spoke
again. "I am sure you have heard stories
about parallel universes where

"everything we say or do is mirrored.
We will not be going outside the pod.
In fact," he said, reaching up and down as

if adjusting controls," I need to be
sure the membrane is intact." I asked, "Do
you mean membrane, as in 'brane theory?'"

"I do. There. I believe everything is
ready. Before I activate the screen,
let me refresh your memory. Matter

"and antimatter will annihilate
if they come into contact. This is why
we are taking extra precautions this

"time. Physicists are spending a lot of
effort investigating dark matter
and dark energy, but they are missing

"the enormous spaces between atoms
and even within atoms. This is where
our parallel universe lies, kept apart

"from our own universe by a membrane.
Let me show you." He waved his arms like a
mime who is pretending to be in a

large box. Immediately I saw, in
color negative, a mirror image
of Master Sun performing the same task

except the image moved left when he moved
right. I could also see a negative
of myself which startled and tried to hide

the same as I did. Master Sun swept the
image aside, as on a cell phone. Then
I could see a negative image of

my neighborhood, and my house. Then he zoomed
in and I could see the inside of my
house, except that it was neat as a pin.

I asked, "Can we affect things that happen
over there?" "Yes." "Can they influence things
that happen over here?" "Yes. Consciousness

"can cross the membrane without causing an
annihilation of either matter
or antimatter. However, objects

"cannot be moved across the membrane, as
they moved on the silicon planet, without
causing the object to annihilate."

Then when he adjusted the screen I watched
a negative-colored world zoom past, as
if we were on an airplane. We touched down

on a beautiful red, mountainous land
with deep valleys that were probably green.
He adjusted the screen again until

we could see what appeared to be the Great
Wall of China. Slowly floating over
the length of it, he said, "This is the part

"of the Great Wall which I built." I could hear
a little bit of pride escape from him.
For some reason it caught me off guard. "I

"directed dozens of men who built the
packed earth structure according to my strict
instructions." Now that part didn't surprise

me. "We planned the ramparts so that signal
fires could be seen from one rampart to
the next, warning stationed troops that there were

"enemies approaching." I asked, "Would it
be possible to go back in time to
when it was built?" He responded, "Space-time

"can be manipulated, but only
to a limited extent. Time travel
actually occurs in our memories.

"Whenever we remember something that
occurred in the past, we are actually
reliving the event. And when we learn

"about a historical event from
books, or movies, or listening to some
narrative and then imagine ourselves

"in that time and place, our consciousness is
engaging in time travel." "But what if
the narrative is wrong?" I asked. He said

"The narrative is never wrong because
in some universe or some other time
dimension, things really happened that way."

He closed the screen and started up the pod.

Canto X

The Anunnaki

"Pilgrim, we will have to return to our
learning base to give you another rest
from deep space exposure. May I?" He took

my head in his hands and looked into my
eyes, then felt my neck as a physician
would do. Quickly examining my hands

and handgrip he said, " Everything looks well,
but I do not want to extend your risk
more than necessary." Then he turned back

to the pod's unseen controls and again
I watched star clusters and galaxies whiz
by. "We are lucky. The Anunnaki

"have agreed to meet us at the learning
base rather than make us fly out to meet
them. It also makes my navigation

easier because they are always on
the move." "Who are the Anunnaki?" I
asked. "They are a great race of travelers

"who have visited many peoples in
many parts of the universe. They have
founded colonies on other planets

"and have guided the evolution of
several civilizations — humans
included — with their gene experiments."

I hesitated, then said, "Um, I'm not
sure I approve of that…" "I agree that
it is invasive, but over the last

"several millennia their laws and
their philosophy have changed to passive
observation. They have developed a

"tremendous respect for the consciousness
within other living beings and they
strive to offer guidance only when it

"is requested. Now I realize that
I have been encouraging you to share
your thoughts and feelings, but this is one time

"when I will have to ask you to maintain
strict silence in their presence. Are you all
right with that?" "Yes, Master Sun." He set

the pod back down on the pleasant learning
area which seemed to have become our
base camp. Stepping out, the air, temperature

and the lovely terrain were very Earth-
like. I could see the small groups of angels
going through their paranormal paces

while Master Sun told me more about the
Anunnaki. Apparently they, too,
had to learn from their mistakes in the past.

He told me about N'biru, their ship,
which was actually more like a planet –
sized spaceship powered by some unknown force.

Apparently, while travelling in deep space,
the Anunnaki hibernate and thus
conserve energy. "That is correct," my

Guide told me. "I am, however, able
to contact Marduk. He is at the helm
for this watch while the others hibernate.

"Then it will be his turn to rest and let
someone else take the helm. Now Pilgrim," he
warned me, "in Babylon, Marduk was a

"great and powerful god who overcame
much opposition from his family
in order to take his throne. In the days

"of Babylon, these gods and goddesses
literally walked among the people.
The temples built to them were actually

"where they lived and the sacrifices of
animals, wine and grains were their meals.
When you first see Marduk, he is very

"imposing. The massive statues in the
temples of Jupiter and Athena
are life-sized representations of two

"of Marduk's siblings who came to Rome. They
went back to N'biru early in the
Etruscan age, but they left such a strong

"impression on later generations
that their status as gods persisted. The
Anunnaki actually began to

"visit Earth and guide the evolution
of humans for hundreds of thousands of
years. That is when Homo Erectus first

"appeared on Earth. Earlier than that, a
different alien race came to Earth
and kick-started the evolution of

"hominids from promising little apes."
I asked, "Will we be meeting that race?" He
shook his head. "Unfortunately, their race

"is now extinct. The only part of them
that still exists is in a few strands of
DNA which humans still carry." "What

"made them extinct?" I asked. Sadly, he shook
his head. "Stupidity. They used up their
resources without replenishing them.

"They failed to control their reproduction
so their DNA became weaker with
each succeeding generation. They could

"not control their aggression, which is what
killed them in the end." I felt that heavy
lead in my gut again. "They sound like the

"human race, don't they?" Sun Wun Liu said,
"As long as a species is alive, it
can change." I stared at him with a feeling .

that I could see apocalyptic sights,
but I wasn't sure if I could trust my
own perception. "Master Sun," I gasped,

"I thought this was supposed to be Heaven.
"Why am I seeing such horror right now?"
"As I told you so very long ago,"

he began, "this Heaven is not what you
have expected. This is the Creation
Realm, and it is vital, while creating,

"to see the evil along with the good."
He gently waved his hand and the visions
went away. "Marduk is waiting for us.

"Remember, people used to worship him.."

Canto XI

Marduk

Sun Wun Liu's last statement to me was
an obvious warning to keep my mouth
shut. It was easier not said than not

done when I first looked inside a temple-
like structure which resembled pictures I'd
seen of the Temple of Jupiter in

Rome. The giant who sat on the throne at
the rear of the grand hall also looked like
someone out of a history book. He

had the curly hair and beard and also
the four wings and sandaled feet that are
on depictions of him from ancient scrolls

and wall friezes. Master Sun bowed deeply.
So did I. A huge voice said, "Sandalphon,
we are honored. You may come forward with

"your student. Sit." "Great Marduk, the honor
is ours. We are here to learn about your
sojourn on Earth." "This is an Earthling then?

"And a living one?" Marduk appeared to
be inhaling my scent, which made me feel
quite nervous. "I have not smelled one of these

"creatures for many ages. It brings back
many memories." He paused to recall
some distant recollection. It seemed like

a long time before he spoke again, but
then he was, indeed, very old. "My brothers
and I built navigation devices

"throughout Sumeria, Egypt, parts of
the Americas. There was that tragic
flood which N'biru precipitated

"because of its gravitational force
on the oceans. Noah and several
other individuals across the

"globe built large arks and were able to save
enough species to repopulate the
world. We Anunnaki realized then

"that we had to leave the Earth and pull our
N'biru far enough away so that
it would no longer disturb Earth's balance.

"But our Homo Sapiens creation
still needed help, so we ordered Yahweh
to stay behind while we watched from a safe

"distance. Unfortunately, Yahweh was
not as spiritually mature as we had
thought. Throughout the Old Testament he would

"smite anyone who made him unhappy.
He favored a few and referred to them
as his chosen people. And then when he

"didn't like their sacrifices or when
he felt unappreciated or when
he decided that they were worshipping

"other gods, he would smite them again. We
realized that Yahweh needed to be
controlled better, so many times we sent

"prophets to bolster the peoples' courage
while we worked privately with Yahweh. The
Buddha was sent to teach people about

"their inner lives and how to connect with
the Great Creator through meditation.
Jesus Christ was sent to teach a newer

"testament of love and of life after
life. By then the people were so jaded
that they crucified him. Mohammed was

"sent to teach how worldly concerns about
business, dealing with hostile neighbors and
such could still be integrated into

"a godly life." An involuntary
gasp at the blasphemy escaped from me,
and Master Sun elbowed me to keep me

quiet. "On occasion some would offer
us a human sacrifice," said Marduk,
taking another whiff of me. "It was

"a nice treat, but the other meats tasted
better." I graciously took the hint. The
former god then talked about how they used

the Egyptian pyramids as beacons
for navigation and how they had learned
the hard way that they needed to dock their

mothership, N'biru, far away from
Earth and commute in with much smaller craft.
He shared with us that he was twenty four

thousand years old, and judging by the way
his mind wandered from one memory to
another, I figured it was the truth.

Marduk shared a bit about some of the
other galactic civilizations
they were monitoring and some of their

interesting life forms. He stated that
life is everywhere and he agreed with
some of our terrestrial scientists

that, given the chemical building blocks,
it is almost impossible for life
not to exist. He talked about forms of

DNA which have different backbones
besides carbon based sugars and he told
us about right spiraled versus left hand

genetic material. And, of course,
he spoke about the consciousness force and
how ubiquitous it is. He expressed

concern about our carelessness with our
own planet and our sloppy handling of
nuclear energy. Then he described

a nuclear war which he and other
Anunnaki waged here on Earth around
twenty-five hundred BC. Startled, I

didn't really mean to raise my eyes to
his, my mouth agape, but I couldn't help
it. "You look surprised, mortal Earthling," he

said. "It was a very foolish little
"war waged by jealous siblings over an
insignificant little planet, and

"fortunately it was a limited
nuclear exchange. But there are still signs
of the conflict around the old Kingdom

"of Ur. Some of the sands there are still fused
into glass. By default we did teach Man
how to fire their pottery, but our

"race has been much more conscientious since
then about handling our disputes calmly."
Marduk shifted a bit in his mighty

throne. "Will there be anything else?" he asked.

Canto XII

a chastisement, taking a break

By this time I was getting excited
about all of this space travel. It was
almost like playing video games or

watching one of the Star Treks. "Where to next?"
I chirped brightly. There was an unhappy
look on Sun Wun Liu's face as he reached

for various invisible dials
on the invisible bulkheads of our
invisible pod. "Master Sun?" I tried

again. He snapped at me, "This is not some
sort of sci fi theme park!" More quietly
he muttered, almost to himself, "Perhaps

"instead of showing you some more funny
aliens I should go over a few
mathematical proofs which can show you

"the mystery of numbers, or I can
show you some natural phenomena
which are unmistakably divine." "I'm

"sorry, Master Sun," I began. Again
with irritation in his voice he snarled,
"This is not a movie about conflicts

"between warring planets.." "I didn't mean
any…" "DO NOT INTERRUPT ME!" I snapped
into silence and bowed my head humbly,

not understanding what I had done wrong.
Master Sun, I could tell, was staring at
me with great intensity. "We have not

"yet seen the Beings of Light," he softly
sighed, almost to himself. I stayed quiet.
The pod seemed to be moving again. "You

"were raised," he said at last, "in a time of
instant miracles with special effects.
I am hoping that your mission with me

"and with Master Alighieri will
not become another technicolor
video game or motion picture. Your

"mission," he raised his hand to silence me,
"is to remember everything you have
seen and put it into writing." I looked

at him fearfully and wanted to tell
him that I'm not any good at writing.
"You will be able to write this story.

"You just have to sit down and do the work.
This was the mission given to Master
Alighieri when he went through his

"voyage, and now it is yours. It may seem
like you have memories from several
days to recall and record, but time is

"a variable thing and you will see
that this entire journey has only
taken a few hours of your time. This

"time compression makes it imperative
that you pay close attention. There is so
much I need to show you. We will have to

"stay close by. Perhaps with the beginners.
And no, I am not angry with you. You
may speak if you wish." I didn't wish to.

So I bowed and watched a few stars whiz by.
"May I ask a question?" I asked him with
as much humility as possible.

"Yes." "Where are we going?" I asked. "I'm scared."
Master Sun looked sadly at me, saying,
"It's not where we are going, but what we

"are travelling toward, like a student
who is walking from a science classroom
to a math classroom. We have been leaping

"across the galaxy by way of
d planets
which can teach us a great deal about the

unique and beautiful ways consciousness
reveals itself..." His voice droned dreamily
while I fought to stay awake. I thought I

could feel the pod touch down again, but I
wasn't sure. Then I looked again into
the face of Enoch who, along with Sun

Wun Liu, seemed to be examining
me or something. "Sarah," Enoch's voice hummed.
Then I heard him say something to Master

Sun on the order of, "You did the right
thing bringing her back." And I fought to stay
awake... stay awake... I wanted to ask

if something was wrong but instead I found
myself aware of a familiar
warm, pillowy soft and feathered body

surrounding mine. "Uh, oh," I muttered. "Am
I dead?" "Not yet," came a voice from outside
Anandiel's wings. I heard a few more

voices outside my beloved feather
bed talk about 'space sickness'. Suddenly
a bolt of pain tore through my head and down

my spine that was so sudden and severe
that I cried out. Enoch's voice said, "Thank you,
Anandiel. You may return now." "No!"

I screamed in pain. "I need him! The pain! Help
me..." As Anandiel slowly vanished
the blinding light, which made the pain so much

worse, revealed many angels around me.
They seemed to be doing a laying on
of hands type healing or something. Their light

dimmed as my pain began to fade. Slowly
I became aware that we were back at
the home base with Enoch, several of

his students and Sun Wun Liu. "Are you
feeling better?" asked my Guide. Enoch seemed
to be coaching his angels on how to

regenerate their own power after
a healing exercise. "What happened?" I
asked. Still woozy I heard Master Sun say,
"You've had a bit of a setback, but you
will be all right." "What do you mean – setback?"
"It is something called 'space sickness'. Even

"with the protection of the pod, it is
difficult to avoid completely. I
have been monitoring you all along

"and it looks like early intervention
was an effective strategy." "Can I
sue you for malpractice?" I asked. Master

Sun said, "There aren't any lawyers up here."

Canto XIII

a hiatus

Convalescence wasn't unpleasant, but
it was frustrating. By this time I was
eager to see more, but Enoch and Sun

Wun Liu had grounded me. About a
dozen student angels helped me pass the
time with soothing massages, stories from

their own past lives and things they learned in
class. The two archangels had left our small
group alone while they went off somewhere to

do whatever it is that archangels
do when they get together. One of my
Three H's, as I called them – Helmsworth, Hank

and Huang – said to me, "You must be a
really important person back on Earth
to have earned this special dispensation

from Above. I mean, *two* archangels are
showing you around the spiritual
realms of Creation." Their continued touch

therapy had strengthened me enough to
sit up. "Actually," I replied, "I'm not
sure why I'm here. I'm not anybody

"in particular. Master Sun has said
something about writing all of this down
but I'm not a writer. I'm not even

"much of a reader." Chloe, always the
cheerleader, piped up, "We can never know
the mind of God. Praise God!" I couldn't help

but growl back at her, "Every time I hear
someone say that I think that another
desperate soul is enabling a

"deity who is not making sense." Her
mouth dropped and I was feeling too queasy
to argue with anyone. I just kind

of tuned her out when she went into an
eight minute rant about faithlessness and
sin and such. I looked around quickly. No

archangels were nearby. Neither were there
any upperclassmen. It should have been
safe to ask a dangerous question. "Um,

"I was wondering about something." One
of the Three H's said, "What would that be?"
I was still reluctant to ask, but all

of the student angels were looking at
me expectantly. "Um, well, I was kind
of wondering if any of you get

"the feeling that nobody is really
in charge?" Marta looked shocked. "Do you mean like
God?" "Well, yeah." Chloe gasped, "You mean after

"seeing all of this," she waved her hand across
the landscape, "you still don't believe in God?"
I felt somewhat defensive. "I believe,

"of course. It's just that God, well, sometimes seems
a bit, you know, incompetent." "Sarah!"
cried Chloe. "That's blasphemy! You'll get sent

"back to Hell!" After being kidnapped by
Whichever Powers That Be and dragged through
Hell and Purgatory myself, I was

in no mood to argue with a rookie
who used to work in Public Relations —
a career inherently designed to

naively manipulate the image
of one's employer. Irritated, I
said, "So you mean that several Earthly

"governments allow free speech, but Heaven
doesn't?" "It's not that," she replied, "it's more
like showing respect." "And not pissing off

"God," I countered. My head still hurt from my
bout with space sickness, whatever that is.
There was another one of those shudders.

Simon, who used to be a weather man,
slumped dejectedly where he sat and said,
"Atmospheric CO_2 just passed the

"tipping point. It's over four hundred now."
Marta looked scared. Chloe looked like she was
plumbing the depths of her denial to

find more excuses and cover-ups. The
guys grumbled about situations they
didn't create. Marta just shivered. Hank

said, "It's like they're expecting us to clean
up this mess. I don't know how to do that."
All of us nodded in agreement. "It's

"just the eighth day of creation," Chloe
sang out nervously. Helmsworth glumly said,
"Why weren't the first seven days good enough?"

Helmsworth then mused, "Sometimes it seems like we're
nothing but God's amusing little ant
farm. Send in a flood and see if the ants

"can swim. Crush a few of us underfoot
and see if the others even try to
retrieve the corpses." Simon rolled his eyes

saying, " Looks like someone forgot to take
his antidepressant today." At that
even Helmsworth chuckled along with the

rest. Marta, the shy one, reflected a
bit. "I thought I had conquered my doubts in
Purgatory, but I keep backsliding.

"I don't know if I'm able to be an
angel." Huang silently nodded. Hank
said softly, "I thought the firewall was

"supposed to purify us so that we
never have moments of weakness any
more." Then Helmsworth: "I'm just relieved to know

"that I'm not the only one who feels this
way. I thought for sure that they were going
to send me to Hell or something because

"I can't seem to meet their expectations."
Huang spoke up, "I come from a culture
where expectations were so high that I

"was always afraid of failing. But then
the way to handle that anxiety
was to study harder and work harder.

"Here I don't know what to study or when
the exams will be. I mean, I'm doing
the meditation exercises and

"the prayers and I'm looking over my notes..."
"You've been taking notes?" Chloe demanded.
"Where did you get the paper and pencil?"

"I prayed for it and it magically showed
up." Chloe looked unhappy. "I suppose
I could do that, but I pray for world peace."

"Anybody happen to see any
archangels around?" Nobody had seen
them. "Probably on a coffee break," I

quipped. Hank looked wistful. "I miss coffee," he
said. "There used to be a doughnut shop next
to the train station. Every morning I'd

"get a steaming hot cup of coffee and
a doughnut that was so fresh it was still
warm from the oven, and then I'd catch the

"6:10 into the city." "I miss the
smell of clean sheets fresh from the clothesline," said
Marta. Huang said that he missed having sex

with his wife and even positive
thinking Chloe became a bit misty
eyed when she said she missed her cat. All of

us were looking quite glum when Master Sun
and Enoch returned. "Your auras are so
dull they look like they're going to sputter

"out like old candles. What's up?" "This mortal
here is getting everyone depressed." It
was Chloe who said that, of course. Enoch

looked at us and said, "Let's talk about it."

Canto XIV

group therapy

Sun Wun Liu sat back and let Enoch
do the talking. "So how long have all of
you been here?" Simon replied, "I don't know.

"It's always daytime here. There's no way to
mark time." The meteorologist was
understandably upset about that.

"Do any of you know why Master Sun
and I took a break?" A few trainees in
the group shrugged. "Instead of continuing

"to examine yourselves and understand
what lies within, you've all been telling us
what you think we want to hear. Master Sun

"and I left so that you could feel more free
to vent your complaints." Master Sun gave me
that penetrating look again and said,

"Verbalize your thoughts, Pilgrim." I hunched up
my shoulders, embarrassed, then admitted,
"That's very wise of you." He persisted,

"That was wise of us ... or what?" "Um, either
you two are very wise or else you are
pretending that you know what you're doing."

So far so good. The heavens didn't split
open with peals of thunder and lightning.
"Go on." I looked nervously around the

group. "Well, um, there's this space sickness thing I
seem to have caught because of our travels. And
then there's this Armageddon thing that seems

"to be going on." "Yes, go on." "And, um,
I still feel like a stupid tourist. I
think I was supposed to have reached some sort

"of epiphany by now or something."
With a triumphant smile, Master Sun
announced to the group, "Now this is the kind

"of honesty I expect from all of
you. It is painful and frightening to
confess feelings which may offend someone

"who is important to you. Enoch and
I are important to all of you, are
we not?" Everyone nodded. "After all,

"none of you know your way around here and
without one or both of us, you will be
lost in Eternity." There were frightened

looks on everyone's faces. Master Sun
continued. "You are not only learning
honesty right now, but you are learning

"trust and faith." "Master Sun," Hank said bravely,
"we've all spent several lifetimes learning
that we cannot trust anyone." "Good work,

"Hank," Master Sun replied. "That was honest
and courageous." Then addressing the group,
"How can you know who to trust, and about

"what can you trust them?" Again, blank, frightened
looks from the group. "The word is discernment,
and you will be learning how to discern

"which entities are trustworthy, which ones
are incompetent," he eyed the group with
a teasing smile, "and which entities

"have evil intent. Do you think you can
trust Enoch and myself to teach you this?"
Expressions of doubt were replaced with sighs

of relief. Choe's face brightened as she
opened her mouth to speak. Master Sun held
up his hand. "This is not a good time to

"say, 'I told you so.'" Obediently
her mouth snapped shut. "It is a good thing that
there is no differentiation of

"days here, one from another. That way you
do not become frustrated when you find
how long you have been here and how long it

"takes to perfect oneself. Simon, you left
your Earthly existence twelve years ago."
He gasped. "As they say on Earth, 'Time flies when

"you're having fun'." Nobody laughed. "Oh, come
now," he chided. "Heaven must be a place
of laughter or else it is not Heaven.

"Laughter is one of the habits of those
whose spiritual vibrations are pure
and vigorous." Since I was the member

of the group who had the worse attitude,
I was the one who said, "What if there is
nothing to laugh at?" "Then just laugh," he said.

"In fact, everybody start laughing now."
Master Sun and Enoch started laughing
for no reason and kept laughing. One by

one the students began to join in, and
even I was caught up in the merry
mood. Actually, it did feel quite good.

After awhile when everyone's face
was relaxed and we all enjoyed ourselves
Master Sun resumed, "There are many ways

"to keep one's vibrations up. Gratitude
is a good way to remain energetic.
Concentrating on what you have versus

"what you think you don't have is actually
an exercise in self-discipline which
strengthens your aura. Also remaining

"positive and optimistic in the
face of adversity is not the same
as denial of the reality

"that surrounds you. This type of positive
thinking actually requires effort,
especially when the negative people

"around you become jealous and believe
you are having an easier time of
it than they are. Generosity and giving

"to others raises your spiritual
energy, as does kindness, compassion
and forgiveness. Since all of these habits

"are difficult to generate and to
maintain, talking to others, prayer, faith
and meditation can help you recharge

"your spiritual batteries. Exercise,
rest, faith, hope and love are all important.
Now," he said to the group, "a priest, rabbi

"and Irishman walk into a bar when…"

Canto XV

news from the front

Enoch took his angel trainees to a
different part of the classroom arena,
possibly to get them away from me

and my charming cynicism they
had all come to know and love. Master Sun
smiled at me, saying, "And now, my cheerful

"little ray of sunshine, tell me what is
on your mind." "Is this almost over?" I
asked. "Soon, Pilgrim. Soon." Just then another

group of angel trainees appeared and talked
excitedly about a field trip they
were just returning from. Meanwhile, Enoch's

group formed into what looked like a football
huddle, clasped their hands and disappeared with
a mighty, "HRAH!!" It looked like fun. Master

Sun took my arm and said, "Come on! Let us
join this group that just returned." The new group
of beginner angels greeted us and

continued to chatter. The cluster of
excited students then cleared enough so
that I could see in their midst was a white

tiger! "Master Sun!" "Relax," he said. "That
is Brodziel, and his white tiger life
was one of his favorites." The angel spied

us and shape-shifted into a human
form. "Master Sun," he said with a bow. My
Mentor bowed also and greeted him. "And

"where have you and your students been?" Master Sun
asked. One of Brodziel's students butted
in with an excited, "There's this planet that

"was taken over by robotics that
the carbon lifeforms developed and we
were only allowed to observe from a

"distance because that planet is being
used by upperclassmen to learn how to
quarantine a planet with dangerous

"lifeforms." That student took a time out to
inhale, while a second student, just as
excited, blurted, "Yeah, but we did get

"to see a planet where 'bots were under
control. The planet became polluted
to the point where the carbon lives couldn't

"live there anymore. They made robots that
were programmed with quantum computers and
the programmers were able to insert

"their own minds into the robots!" "That makes
the robots essentially immortal,"
another student interjected, "since

"the 'bots get all of their energy from
sunlight — or rather light from their star." And
another student said, "They can repair

"themselves and create new 'bots with parts from
warehouses…" Then the first student cut in
with, "But they still depend on natural

"resources for plastics and metal parts.
That's the downside." Student Number Two said,
"But the good part is that they can travel

"anywhere in the universe without
the precautions humans need to take, like
with oxygen, extreme temperatures and

"radiation…" he drifted off, glancing
at me, "oh, I'm sorry. I forgot that
you…" Master Sun smiled at him and said,

"It is all right. My human Pilgrim is
quite understanding. Is she not?" He dug
his elbow into my ribs. "Yes!" I yelped.

"Tell me about your robot planet. I
probably won't get to visit it," one
more jab. "Um, we're on a strict time schedule."

He smiled. Brodziel asked his three, "Are
robots truly alive?" "Do you mean they're
not?" This was asked by the first student, who

had been a math teacher once. "I'm asking
you," Brodziel returned. "Can machines be
truly alive? Do they have thoughts? If so

"when do they change from being a product
of a sentient being to really
being sentient themselves?" The second

student, a former mechanic, said, "I'm
not sure they can ever be alive, like
a person. I've repaired too many of

"them to believe that machines are able
to think or have feelings like us." The third
student, a nurse, offered, "But they contained

"the minds of their creators, and that mind
is what converted them into living
creatures." Turning to Brodziel, the first

student asked, "By the way, what does happen
to the mind contained within the robot
if the power goes out?" "They appear to

"be stored in memory chips like other
data. Kind of like a calculator
that can remember how to do math when

"the 'on' button is pressed again." "Maybe,"
said the nurse, "a robot cannot really
be alive, but it can be a storehouse

"for consciousness." Always the professor,
Brodziel then asked, "Can a normally
inanimate object remain unchanged

"when a basic force like consciousness is
stored in it? For that matter, do bodies
exert a force on consciousness and change

"it somehow?" "What do you mean?" asked the math
teacher. "For example, changes in the gravitation
force, like space travel, can

"affect a human body's skeletal
muscle and circulatory system.
The consciousness force can change an object

"into a living entity, and when
the consciousness force leaves, the creature dies."
The mechanic said, "I *have* fixed some cars

"that seem to have a mind of their own." "Like
my old SUV," laughed the first student.
The angelic professor asked him,

"*Did* your car have a mind of its own?" He
looked flustered. "What do you mean?" Brodziel
again asked, "Did your car have a mind? Did

"you swear at it? Did you give it a name?"
Now the student really seemed embarrassed.
"It's OK," said the angel. "It's normal

"for people to talk to their cars. After
all, the drive to and from work sometimes takes
more of one's day than family time does."

He finally admitted that all of
the above was true, his SUV's name
was SuzyQ, and he talked to the car.

"Perhaps SuzyQ had consciousness."

Canto XVI

conscious things

Brodziel told the group "What I'm saying
is that it is possible to transfer
consciousness to inanimate objects.

"Humans are not very good at this, but
some legends of magic swords and crystals
and such are based in fact. These objects, though,

"are sort of like magnets that can lose their
charge after awhile. There are psychics
who can pick up conscious energy

"from a person's possessions. And there are
objects that can hold curses." I shuddered
at the thought of haunted stuff. Brodziel

noticed my discomfort, saying, "The old
legends also talk about specially
blessed objects and protective amulets."

"Who does the blessing and cursing?" I asked.
He replied, "Intercessions through prayer,
sometimes groups of humans, like covens, can

"ritually charge an object, sometimes
consciousness can be stored in areas
that are considered sacred and objects

"can be charged there. I hear that Master Sun
has shown you other planets and other
dimensions where consciousness manifests

"in ways that we are not accustomed to." My
Guide and Mentor let me answer, "Yeah." I
hesitated, looking back at him. The

students smiled expectantly. I told them
about the silicon planet and the
parallel universe and the planet

where evolution proceeded in a
different direction from Earth's. "Did you
see the neural network on the ocean

"floor?" asked one of them. I indicated
a 'no'. The student added, "The oceans
on Earth have microorganisms that

"cover the bottom and they are able
to communicate with each other in
an unusual way." "Yes," said the nurse.

"It's almost like a massive brain within
the sea." The mechanic said eagerly,
"It's all like some sort of Mandelbrot set.

"Life keeps repeating itself in patterns
that replicate themselves, too. Consciousness
is kind of like God or something." "God is

"consciousness and more," Brodziel added.
"God is the consciousness that resides in
all living creatures. Creativity

"is God. The act of creation is God.
The rules that control natural science
are God. God is an equation and God

"is mathematics itself. Yet God is
also whatever we need God to be
whenever we are lonely or in pain.

"God is the essence of relationships
we have with each other and God is love.
God is also destruction of the old

"to make way for the new, much as Shiva,
Vishnu and Brahma work in partnership.
Reincarnation and evolution,

"death, conception, procreation, rebirth
are all parts of the mystery of God.
Primal instincts and higher consciousness,

"learning and even forgetting are God.
Space and time are God. Every universe
has been created and governed by God.

"Our memories, our aptitudes, our skills
are part of God and return to God when
we depart our living Earthly body.

"The same is true of every living thing
throughout the many universes that,
within their many body types, have lived

"and learned and loved and reproduced and died.
This is how God renews Itself through time.
We are all God and God is all of us."

I mused, "I keep hearing that theme over
and over again. It's both exciting
and frightening. It puts so much on my

"shoulders. I mean, if I am part of God,
there is so much responsibility.
I have to monitor myself at all

"times and keep my thoughts, words and actions pure.
And when I die I have to contribute
everything I've learned in life to the God

"force, like my experiences are some
sort of nourishment or something. I can't
do it all." Brodziel turned to Sun Wun

Liu saying, "I think she's getting it."
"Huh?" Master Sun stepped in. "You do not
have to do it all. This is where you learn

"to trust others, work with others and pray
to the Divine Creator for guidance
from those who can help you. All of us are

"interconnected, like brain cells or like
qubits in a quantum computer, or
like a flock of birds who migrate in a

"large group. We need each other and we need
divine guidance to lead us to those who
can help us rather than harm us. You are

"correct in knowing that our paths are not
easy, but you still need to learn how much
easier our paths are to travel when

"we choose not to walk alone." I argued,
"But other people can be such a pain.
They're mean, stupid, gossipy and pushy."

"So are you, Pilgrim," he said. "So are you."

Canto XVII

chatting with the students

The class chattered about entropy
and how it can be reversed when going
through a black hole during the creation

of a new universe. A few student
angels even debated while scribbling
equations. Other students asked about

the probability of Krebs cycles
for nitrogen rather than oxygen
and wondered what the reducing agent

would be. Still others shared their interviews
with the hundred forty-four thousand host
from the twelve tribes of Israel, none of whom

were Jehovah's Witnesses. (I made it
a point to ask.) Their conversation turned
to the concepts of how to create a

universe and which skill sets one would need
if one wanted to be God. "Isn't that
a bit heretical?" I asked. "I don't

"think it is," came one reply. "OK, then,"
I persisted, "how about presumptuous?"
The same student angel replied, "Not if

"you want to become God it's not." "I guess
it's good to have goals," I muttered. "OK,
so which skills do we need if we are to

"become gods?" There weren't any archangels
or upperclassmen around, so I felt
that the ensuing discussion should be

entertaining, if nothing else. In truth,
I was getting bored. Sun Wun Liu was
running off with Enoch, Brodziel and

some other archangel who had us sit
for his five angel trainees. "I think God
needs to be all-wise and all-loving," said

one of the recent additions to our
group. "That's quite original," I proclaimed.
Another student from that same group said

eagerly, "We'd have to be able to
create something out of nothing. You know
like the Big Bang." "Or," I surmised, "like a

"single mom feeding her kids." The nurse from
Brodziel's group snickered and added, "Been
there, done that. I guess that means I'm a

"goddess already." The second newbie
from What's-His-Name's group didn't quite get the
joke, saying, "Yeah, but are you all-knowing

"all-seeing and able to create life?"
Hank, from Enoch's group chuckled and replied,
"Nancy was a nurse in her previous

"two lives. The only thing she can't do is
balance her bank accounts." Nancy punched him
in the shoulder. "But then again, we don't

"have any banks around here." Said Nancy,
"Good thing or we'd both be getting foreclosed."
"OK, then," the previous student (named

Roger) declared. "It would be vital for
a god to be able to do math." A
student from What's-His-Name's group named Shelby

grunted slightly and muttered, "You'll have to
excuse Roger. He graduated from
Purgatory because his father

"built a cathedral somewhere." Then turning
toward Roger he added, "I believe
that the Divine Creator is the One

"who *invented* mathematics. And all
of the laws of Physics, Chemistry and
Biology. And the very fabric

"of space-time." Someone named Wanda scolded
him, "Shelby, the Divine Creator would
also have complete self-control or else

"It wouldn't be the universal force
of everything that's good." Shelby sort of
growled under his breath, "I'm getting sick of

"all this self-control. I want a beer." I
liked Shelby. I was about to make his
acquaintance when Serapres (formerly

known as What's-His-Name) appeared along with
a couple more archangels. There were just
too many names to remember, you

know? Serapres plopped his hand on Shelby's
shoulder and said, "Come on, Buddy, let me
buy you a beer." As they walked away, one

student asked, "Is he really going to
do that?" Brodziel stated, "Nah, that's just
his way of announcing that it's time for

"a correctional interview. So what
were you all discussing while we were gone?"
Roger chimed, "We were figuring out what

"we need to become God." I muttered, "A
heart, a brain and courage." My mood became
blacker by the minute, wondering when

this state of limbo was going to end.
Then an angel trainee named Patty said,
"Wait a minute. Aren't you the mortal who

"went through Hell and Purgatory so that
you could save humanity?" "Um, not quite…"
"Sure! I could tell you were mortal," she gushed.

"Oh, Sarah," exclaimed Roger, "I think it's
wonderful that you agreed to go through
Heaven, Hell and Purgatory just

"so you could write it all down and save mankind!"
"Huh? Where did you hear...?" Then Patty: "All of
us have been watching you, and we all prayed

"for you and Dante when you were in Hell..."
"Huh?" "...and we were all so delighted when
you and Anandiel decided to

"go through the firewall..." "Huh?" "...and we are
all so proud of you for deciding to
give humanity a badly needed

"message of hope!" They all nodded gaily.
Dumfounded, I said, "Really, I didn't
agree to any of this..." "God bless you,

"Sarah! God bless you!" and Patty fluttered
off somewhere. The others excitedly
congratulated me on my mission.

Not wanting to utter any swear words
in the Heavenly Realms, I just said, "Poop."
Trying to be supportive, Nancy said,

"You were predestined — just like the prophets!"
"All right, Spooks, listen up." Deathly silence.
"I DON'T BELIEVE IN PREDESTINATION!"

I didn't mean to yell like that. My words
literally rang through the heavens. Some
students left quietly. Some left, angry.

Sun Wun Liu stepped in just then. As he
pulled me aside, I could hear someone say,
"Uh oh. A correctional interview."

I just rolled my eyes and said, "Whatever."

Canto XVIII

a heartfelt chat

There was that awkward silence as my Guide
and I strolled deliberately toward
a lovely orchard far away from the

group. In silence he and I surveyed the
beautiful landscape, more lovely than the
Earthly paradise in Purgatory.

I could hear in the distance that mighty
'HRAH!' that implied the joyful departure
of Enoch's group for another field trip.

"How well do you know the Old Testament?"
Master Sun said finally. "Just what I
learned in Sunday School," I confessed. I felt

ashamed and embarrassed at my failure
to keep up my Bible reading. "Are you
familiar with the story of the

"two sacrifices? One bull was for Baal.
His four hundred fifty priests were to cut
up the bull and pray for Baal to accept

"it without lighting a fire on the
altar. Alone, I did the same for the
God of Israel. I had my servants pour

"gallons and gallons of water on the
sacrifice plus the altar and the wood.
Then we all prayed. Only my sacrifice

"was accepted when God sent fire from
above, consuming the wet offering.
The four hundred fifty priest were outdone,

"of course. But that was not enough. I had
all of them killed." He looked away and fell
silent again. "Master Sun?" I questioned,

"what are you saying?" He just shook his head.
"Metatron appears to his students as
Enoch, to shield them from his archangel

"intensity, as do all the other
instructors. I come to you as Sun Wun
Liu because I hate my lifetime as

"Elijah." "Master Sun!" I didn't know
which shocked me more, the announcement itself
or his sudden vulnerability.

Despite the conversational lull, I
remained silent. After a time he
said, "The Old Testament only gives hints,

"but after that slaughter, I spent the rest
of my priesthood in mourning. And then there
was more slaughter, but I remained faithful

"to Yahweh. I prayed daily, asking for
forgiveness for all the bloodshed. By
Yahweh's decree. Bloodshed. Finally the

"Divine Creator took pity on me,
passed my mantle onto Elisha, and
took me in the fiery chariot."

He seemed so sad that I couldn't help but
ask, "Can I give you a hug?" Suddenly,
Sun Wun Liu sprouted outstretched wings and

towered over the trees — a hundred feet
tall. "I DO NOT NEED A HUG," he thundered.
"I AM TRYING TO TEACH YOU SOMETHING." Then

just as suddenly, he was Master Sun
again, and he said softly, "You may come
out now. It is safe." I thought I could hear

a couple of familiar angel
voices in the other grove laughing their
guts out, but I wasn't sure. "Come, sit down,"

he said in his usual calm voice. "The
point I am trying to make is that, if
you think you feel disillusioned with the

"way the universe is run, well, so have
I. If you feel guilty about someone
you have harmed, I feel that guilt

"a hundred-fold. And as far as Roger
is concerned, he was once a brilliant
scientist who helped create the atom

"bomb. He still despises his intellect

so much that he pretends it is not there.
You are not the only one who has had

"his or her heart broken when you only
meant to do the right thing. All the other
students have their stories to tell. Do you

"understand?" I nodded. "Are you ready
to return to the class area?" "Yes."
He and I chatted about nothing in

particular as we made our way back.
The other students were gone, probably
on another one of their excursions.

Enoch greeted us and Master Sun said,
"Wait for me over there," and he pointed
to one of my favorite spots nearby.

I heard Enoch's voice say, "Sure you couldn't
have chosen a better one?" And I heard
Master Sun, "It was not my choice to make."

I stood and waited for him nervously.

Canto IX

the choice

Master Sun told me to sit down, then he
sat opposite me. "There is one last
place I wish I could show you," he said, "but

"the choice, as always, is entirely
up to you. At any time you can end
this journey. All you have to do is tell

"me and I will return you safely to
your familiar home. You have endured a
great deal and your courage has been noticed

"by many souls that you have not even
met." "This doesn't sound good," I said. "Your sense
of humor has been appreciated,

"too." "How 'bout my lousy attitude?" (I
couldn't resist. Master Sun had not been
properly flirted with up to that point.)

He was quite serious. "What I am going
to offer you could cost you your Earthly
life. After your last bout of space sickness,

"your body was weakened to the point where
you can take one more trip in the pod, but
only if your entire will and your entire

"being can embrace this last trip." I looked
at him expectantly. He resumed, "At
the firewall and the two rivers you

"caught a glimpse of the ecstasy which is
Heaven. But you have not witnessed the bliss
which has been spoken of by mystics and

"saints throughout history and all over
the world. Dante tried to describe it and
even he confessed, in his *Comedy*,

"that he could not find the words. What I am
offering to introduce you to are
the Beings of Light." Of course, I asked who

the Beings of Light are. "They are the most
advanced entities from all over the
universe. In fact, they are able to

"ascend to the Divine Creator, then
descend back down to us archangels in
order to communicate. Some of them

"are awaiting final acceptance to
return to the body of the Divine
Creator, while others choose to remain

"as communicators. They do not have
physical bodies any longer, since
they have perfected their spirit, their will

"and their consciousness to the point where they
can manifest without physical forms."
I asked, "Why don't they manifest on the

"Earthly plane where they could do a lot of
good?" He answered, "Their energy is too
strong. In fact, I will be fortifying

"the usual shields in the pod for your
protection. Even with the extra shields…"
his voice drifted off. I thought I could hear

a slight crack in his voice. "What will I gain
by seeing these beings?" He sighed and turned
his face back to me. "It will give you an

"unshakeable sense of purpose. They are
so pure and filled with divine love that
one's life is invariably changed. The

"desire to reunite with the One
of Creation rules one's existence and
leads to incredible bliss." "Would it be

"dangerous?" "For you, yes." "Can I meet them
from a distance or something?" "I can try
to describe them and their power as best

"I can." I thought for a moment and said,
"But it's not the same as actually
meeting them, huh?" "Correct." "If they're so pure

"and holy and all that, can't they protect
me from themselves?" Master Sun: "Already
they know about you and your journey. They

"have prepared themselves thoroughly, but
you are mortal and you were so weakened
by first a nuclear blast and then by

"space sickness, and we haven't had enough
time to let you recuperate fully.
The decision to return home or to

"fulfill your mission is such a daunting
one that I shall recruit some help for you.
Anandiel," he called while looking past

my right shoulder. Instantly, my blessed
friend and guardian materialized.
We hugged and didn't even notice that

Sun Wun Liu had left us alone. "Oh,
Anandiel, what should I do?" "I am
not the one who is able to decide.

"All I can do is tell you about our
options and then stay close to you no
matter what your decision is. " I asked

him, "Do you know anything about these
Beings of Light?" "I only know as much
as you do." "Do you think I'll die if I

"go to see them?" He answered, "I can give
you a probability of fifty-
fifty." "Well, that sucks." "Yeah, it does. But then

"we've both seen the life after life, so death
seems to be part of a continuum."
The ground shuddered again. Anandiel

said sadly, "That was another terror
attack. This time Russia and the U.S.
are priming their missiles and making their

"ambassadors work overtime again."
Clutching his neck I cried out, "I'm so scared
Anandiel!" Holding me gently, he

said, "So is everyone else on Earth. They
need to keep their spiritual energy
high and not descend into hopelessness.

"They need to know that there is an end game.
They need to learn how to pray, meditate
and turn to each other for support.

"They need hope, love and courage to face what
lies ahead. I think we both cherish our
fellow struggling souls." With a sigh I said,

"Well then, let's go see what the big deal is."

Canto XX

the beings of light

Anandiel held my trembling hand as
Sun Wun Liu adjusted dials on
his invisible pod walls again. This

time he made me and Anandiel sit
on form-fitting lounge chairs like those made for
astronauts. He also took a lot more

time fussing with the invisible knobs
than he had taken before. *And* he hooked
me up to some sort of monitor which

he insisted was necessary if
I were to travel in the pod again.
"Why didn't you take these safeguards before?"

I asked. I didn't mean to accuse him
of anything, I was just wondering.
"Forgive me, Pilgrim," he answered with some

irritation. "While you were destroying
the confidence of Enoch's students, he
and I were engineering improvements

"in this ship." "I'm sorry," I muttered, "I
didn't mean anything, I just wondered…"
"S-S-H-H! I am trying to concentrate," he

said while fine-tuning something I couldn't
see. "All right. Are you ready?" I nodded.
"Anandiel? Are you ready?" He, too,

nodded. I couldn't detect any change
in the pod, except that stars were flying
past like snowflakes in the headlights

of a car that is driving in a storm.
I *was* feeling a bit dizzy but I
didn't want to ruin the trip by saying

anything. However, Master Sun turned
to Anandiel and made some sort of
hand motion. My guardian angel felt

my forehead and checked my pulse and breathing,
then gave an OK sign to Master Sun.
Suddenly, we arrived at a place of

indescribable beauty! Shimmering
light waves caressed a golden city which
cannot be compared with any on Earth.

This is the point where even Dante was
at a loss for words. The new Creation!
The magnificence! The blessed new world

which John of Patmos could only describe
as, "the new Heaven and the new Earth, for
the old Heaven and the old Earth had passed

'away." It was a new Eden which I
could tell was populated only by
enlightened, refined individuals

whose very existence exuded LOVE!
Dante tried to describe spheres of planets.
I now cannot describe wonders of space.

This had to be the city described in
Revelation, the one ruled by Jesus
for a thousand years with peace – devoutly

prayed for, desired, wished for, heavenly
peace! And the beings – yes – Beings of Light
they were indeed! Surrounding us with love.

Then, sure enough, I believe I passed out.
When I opened my eyes again I felt
Anandiel nearby and LIGHT ⸱ so much

light from so many beings surrounding
us, infused with a peace and a love I
had never known before. They had healed me!

"Master Sun, how can I possibly let
you know how grateful I am to you, to
Dante and to everyone else I've met

"for everything all of you have taught me?"
"Remember and write," said Sun Wun Liu.
"Remember and write. Remember and write.

"There have been such marvelous advances
in our knowledge base and applications
of that knowledge. But all of our holy

"books are ancient. Many people believe
that there is no room in science for God.
Others cling so firmly to the ancient

"books that they think God does not believe in
science. Especially now, during the
dawning of the eighth day of creation

"it is so important that all of these
people are brought back to the Infinite
in order to draw strength for themselves and

"their loved ones. Many changes will occur
and as I have told you before, changes
can be frightening. Remember and write."

Then he grew solemn. "You have the option
of staying here, I need to tell you this."
I savored the bliss of the Enlightened

Ones. "If you stay, you will indeed possess
the eternal bliss you see here, but the
energy is so powerful that you

"must shed your mortal body if you are
to enter it." Again I drank in the
holy splendor and the pure energy.

The connectedness, the blessed feelings
reawakened that old longing within
me for peace and blissful rest. I asked him,

"If I go back, will the chronic pain still
be there?" "Yes." "Will I have better rapport
with that heartache that was supposed to be

"family?" "It depends on what you put
into it." "Will I be publicly shamed
if I share what I've seen and heard over

"here?" "Probably." I gazed at the crystal
city and the pure, joyful spirits who
danced around it. I remembered all of

my best efforts that resulted in such
humiliating failures. I could see
again the faces of everyone who

hated me and everything I stood for.
Some of them, the ones who thought they were kind,
politely turned their backs. Some demanded

that I be medicated. Some were rude.
"Will you be nearby so I can call on
you?" "Anandiel and I will always

"be at your side. You will not see us but
you will feel us near you. Pilgrim,
I must be honest. If you go back you

"will suffer as before, and continue
to be judged and misunderstood, and in
the end, you will die just as everyone

"else does. I cannot promise you success
or even satisfaction, but I can
promise all of his," his hand swept over

the blessed vista, "at the end of your
natural life." Then, Master Sun intoned,
"There are many terrified people on

"Earth who do not understand the changes
that are taking place. They turn to drugs and
to cults for solace and are destroyed by

"them. Some religious leaders have given
up and allowed hatred to be sanctioned."
He paused. I contemplated. Then I told

him, "My place is with the people. When they
die in cataclysms, I will die, too."
Then Sandalphon took my head in his hands.

"The blessings of an angel are on you."
"Master Sun?" "Yes, Pilgrim." "There's just one more
thing…" "Yes?" "Um, I would like to see Jesus."

He waved his arms with an immense flourish.
Suddenly, the brightest light I'd ever
experienced, brighter that the blast which

propelled me into Purgatory, filled
the air. Emerging from that holy light
were the figures of a man in pure white

robes with his arms extended as if on
a cross, another man in ancient robes
carrying a staff, and Master Sun — now

appearing as Sandalphon. I knew then
why the apostles wanted to build an
altar during the Transfiguration.

But then, a huge chorus of angels joined
in and Dante, Virgil and so many
others I had met during my journey